THE BRAND BOOK

How to build a profitable brand — fast, effectively and efficiently

THOMAS OOSTHUIZEN

Stonebridge
books

First published by Stonebridge, an imprint of Jacana Media (Pty) Ltd, in 2013

10 Orange Street
Sunnyside
Auckland Park 2092
South Africa
+2711 628 3200
www.jacana.co.za

Email: Thomas@drthomasbrand.co.za
Website: www.drthomasbrand.co.za
Blog: brand-blog.drthomasbrand.co.za
Twitter: @drthomasbrand

ISBN 978-1-920292-14-0

Cover concept by publicide
Design and layout by Breinstorm
Set in Tiempos Text 8/11 pt
Printed by Ultra Litho (Pty) Ltd, Johannesburg
Job no. 001991

See a complete list of Jacana titles at www.jacana.co.za

CONTENTS

PREFACE

This book is aimed at brand owners, company executives, marketers, brand managers and entrepreneurs – big and small. It reflects the experiences that I have built up of how marketing works. I hope it will help you to better build and maintain your brands, and to increase their value – and your profit – through improved marketing.

Marketing is an opportunity cost. Money you spend on advertising could have been spent elsewhere, so you have to make it count. Few companies can waste money; it needs to do the job and to be accountable.

The process that I will explain to you was developed during years of launching and advising on many blue chip brands, notably in the early phases of brands such as Outsurance, Emirates, Vodacom, ABSA, AngloGold Ashanti, eBucks, Tracker and e.tv. Furthermore, it involved years of working on the marketing for brands such as Sasol Oil, Colgate-Palmolive, MTN, Volkskasbank, Ster-Kinekor and National Brands. In the process, I dealt with many amazing clients and colleagues, who taught me a lot.

I know that what I will share with you works. Although much of marketing is up in the air, there are some certainties. I have been in the marketing industry for 25 years. Many of my clients paid my "school fees". Some benefited greatly, most have become friends and some have allowed me to experiment with different thinking – mostly to our mutual advantage.

I will not give away client confidentialities. I will focus on things that have largely become common knowledge over the years, or where incidents in the past no longer matter to the brands. History has the ability to blur the origins of things and in the process to build up one's collective intelligence.

The exponential benefit of great marketing has more power than any other discipline to make a company successful. To do that, we need the right mix of analysis, process, intuition and creativity.

This is a practical, rather than philosophical book – I hope it works for you that way.

ONE

WE FACE A CHANGING
BRAND UNIVERSE

- Brand management is often a hit-and-miss affair
- Most companies use no analysis at all
- Marketing and brand professionals often can't agree about the words we use
- Marketing budgets hardly ever have clear objectives
- Whatever we do in marketing has to "get" and "keep" customers

A rapidly changing world is placing new demands on the developing and building of brands through smart marketing. But many businesses do not seem to be aware of the challenges facing them and simply continue with a hit-and-miss approach.

Sadly, this is very true in marketing, I would say in at least 70% of instances. This results in wasted opportunities. Some research suggests consumers have a less than 10% chance of seeing a new television advertisement.

The marketing of our brands has to be goal directed. All marketing is aimed at retaining and gaining customers – brands are the conduits used to achieve these objectives. This means all marketing activities must be traced back to whether they achieved these objectives. Marketing activities must be systematic and accountable, based on proper analysis. We need to know which factors build – or detract from – the value of our brands. If elements within the brand mix are out of line, it costs money and wastes time. If they are well orchestrated, the exponential benefit to the brand is enormous.

This is even more true in a world where exponential technological advances, especially information and communication technology, have enabled the creation of a global village in which competition for the same markets and resources is continually increasing. A shifting of economic power to China, India and other emerging countries, and a growing awareness of social and environmental issues, adds to the complexity of doing business.

In my experience, much of brand management is a bit of a hit-and-miss affair. Sometimes it works, sometimes it does not. And we do not always know why, so we do not learn from our mistakes. Some will say brand managers at companies change so often that any learning is futile anyway. Yet, if a company builds up its own collective intelligence, this need not be the case.

Although good brand management requires a mix of creativity and analysis, most companies use no analysis at all. That includes companies that spend a lot of money on research.

Most companies have a lot of data, yet few use it. Even fewer companies use their own internal data.

Marketing budgets are hardly ever task-driven with clear objectives.

Within the competitive environment, the strongest competitors are those that leverage resources better than their peers.

In this complex brand environment, all brand owners have to:
- Extract greater value from existing brands and sell more at higher margins;
- Retain existing customers and attract (the right) new customers;
- Create new brands, new markets and new products;
- Make sure that any new brand – or brand extension or innovation – works and delivers profit from the outset; and
- Do all of this with fewer resources.

The process that I will outline should enable brand owners to identify the elements they need to consider when creating, building and managing a brand; to understand how to determine what builds and detracts from a brand; and to realise how these factors relate to one another.

But first of all we should know what we are talking about.

Getting on the same page

I often use the analogy that when a doctor mentions a colon, all other doctors know what he is talking about. There can be no disagreement about what a colon is.

Sadly, this is not true for marketing and brand professionals. We often cannot even agree about the words we use. This undermines our credibility as it looks as though we don't know what we are talking about.

Whatever we do in marketing needs to achieve one of two objectives: to attract more customers and to retain existing customers, of the right profile and at the right profit margin. We want to do that so that we can sell more to the same customers, attract new customers or create new products to sell to existing or new customers. Every single thing we do in marketing needs to be measured by this. (Marketing has to achieve both objectives, but not necessarily simultaneously. It is important to know which objective is most important when. For example, when the economy is bad, keeping your customers may be the most opportune thing to do, because growth may be expensive or almost impossible. Also, if a brand is very big, such as ABSA, keeping customers may take precedence over acquiring them because you will be the target for other brands wanting to acquire your customers.)

Brand management is the most important tool we have to achieve these objectives.

What is a brand?

THESE ARE SOME EXPLANATIONS THAT WORK FOR ME.

 A brand can be defined as a basket of benefits associated with a given name. I like this definition a lot – a brand is shorthand for a set of benefits. The intangible aspect of it is useful, because so much of a brand is not seen or heard but "felt".

It does signify that we are talking about a concept that is largely a construct of individual insights, perceptions and experiences. Therefore, no two people will believe exactly the same thing about a given brand. It is the degree of this difference that we need to manage as marketers. Assuming that we cannot do so, amid the greater consumer liberation today, is not entirely true. Even though we have limitations, we need to be on top of our own brand debate.

Great brands have clear meanings. A brand name is not a random thing. It needs careful crafting to be authentic and sustainable. A brand is sometimes called a maker's mark, to underline its authenticity and origin.

In *Brand Asset Management*, Scott Davis calls a brand a set of promises. He states that consumers associate certain benefits or values with strong brands:
- 3M means innovation;
- Virgin means good value and fighting for the consumer's rights;
- Nike means personal performance;
- Hallmark means caring;
- FedEx means guaranteed delivery.

Over the years, the associations have made these brands strong and they have given consumers reasons to support them. Much of the value contained in these brands is a function of how well defined the value is in the minds of their target-market customers.

A brand is thus a name with a specific meaning. This separates a brand from a product. Whereas all banks may have integrity (or so we hope), not all are uniquely and singularly defined. To me, strong brands are unique. Even though Alessi makes many different kinds of household utensils, they share one trait: they are fun to use.

The value of a brand is often a function of this meaning. The more relevant (to consumer needs) this meaning is, the better, and the more unique (the only brand to offer a particular meaning to the consumer), the greater the value of the brand. An Apple iPhone satisfies the requirement for making a call at its most basic level, like all other handsets, yet it does it in a unique way with incremental meanings, which creates enormous value in the name Apple iPhone.

Strong brands deliver consistent revenue – generally at high profit margins. That is a universal truth about great brands. Whether you enter a McDonald's store in Moscow or in New York, the brand experience will be very similar – even the price paid in relative terms. This consistency creates familiarity across borders, which in turn translates into the global value of the brand. For consumers, it means a consistent experience of the brand meaning, wherever they go.

 A brand defines a template of expectations for the consumers. Within this template of expectations will be what consumers heard, saw or read about it, but this will largely be amplified by the experience they will have when they encounter the brand in real life – for example, when they walk into a store.

In *The Brand Gap*, Marty Neumeier calls a brand a gut feeling about a product, service or company. He states that brands are defined by consumers – and not by companies – and that they have distinctive perceptions. He sees brand management as the management of differences. Differences lead to the reasons why a given brand should be supported above the average offer of the category.

THE ABOVE TELLS US TWO THINGS.

 First, a strong brand consists of a complex set of benefits to the consumers, functional and/or emotional. Much of this is intangible and exists within people. The collective meaning of brands in fact defines them. A Rolex is an expensive watch with significant functional benefits, yet it is also a status symbol because of the collective knowledge of what it is worth. Much of desire is defined within the collective consciousness. Each depends on the other.

Second, a strong brand is clearly differentiated in that it offers the consumer benefits not offered by other brands. In fact, the very word "brand" is about creating a particular set of connotations with a given name. Without it, a brand will also not sustain its profit margins. Once a customer asks, "Why pay more?" the brand has lost its battle for consistent and superior returns.

We have examples of industries where most brands have lost their battle: the American airline industry is largely commoditised. Mostly people simply fly the cheapest one. This undermines the very principle of branding. If the brand name cannot leverage value, it is meaningless. Yet, many brand owners do not understand this.

When friends react in ways we find strange or out-of-character, we try to understand why and we may even ask them what is wrong. Brands are the same: a brand owner needs to know this. A brand is a fragile receptacle of value. Any imbalance in the equation raises questions.

What consistent meaning does your brand have? If you or your brand team cannot answer that in one short sentence, your brand is most likely not doing as well as it could. As with all aspects of management, how can you drive relevant activities and measure results if you do not have a clear understanding of what your brand must be?

What is brand value?

Brand value can be its potential purchase value (should another company want to acquire the brand). It can also be defined as the profit margin the brand is able to earn as measured against other brands in the same product or service class.

The important equation we manage as marketers, whether we are conscious of it or not, is the relationship between perceived value (what consumers believe they get out of our brand) and price (what they pay for the brand). Generally, price is not questioned until the value is questioned.

The job of a marketer is largely to manage the value side of the equation. This value is with customers and with investors.

HOW DO BRAND AND MARKETING FIT TOGETHER?

Marketing is the way in which companies leverage their brands to retain and grow their business. This in turn creates company revenue, profit and asset value.

We market to create business value. The conduit for business value is mostly brand value.

Brand value is created when we produce revenue and margins from customers who buy from the brand. The intention of all marketing is therefore to retain ("to keep") and attract ("to get") customers. In the retention and acquisition we create brand and business value.

The extent to which we can leverage the value of customer relationships will determine how sustainable, profitable and valuable our brands are.

The question of how marketing relates to a brand is therefore to ensure that everything you do in marketing either retains, grows or attracts customers, increases their perception of the brand and increases their perception of the value delivered by the brand. If we do that consistently as marketers, we will create a successful brand with a consistent revenue stream for the brand owner.

So whatever we do in marketing has to "get" and "keep" customers: those are the conduits for successful brands.

TWO

A "RECIPE" FOR BRAND MANAGEMENT

have a horror of recipes. Yet when most brand management is a hit-and-miss affair, even a mediocre recipe may be better than pot-luck.

Although creating, building and maintaining brands cannot be regarded as a recipe to be followed, there are elements that need to be managed to give these processes a better-than-average chance of succeeding.

In this chapter I will introduce the model that I have developed to manage these elements to create and maintain brand value. And in the following chapters I will deal with the most important elements in more depth.

The way I look at brands can be summarised by an equation that I will explain in detail. The essential thesis of this equation is if you add up all the elements that make up a brand and create its equity, there is a multiplier effect for well-managed brands.

Strong brands are built in a sequen- $1+1=3$ tial – and iterative – manner. If the brand elements are aligned, the approach will work. If they are not aligned, it most likely will not work in the long term.

The added advantage of this alignment per area is not simply 1+1=2, but 1+1=3+. This means one element aligned well with the next element will create exponential advantage to the brand owner. In the same way, a badly aligned element will detract from the brand and make 1+1=1 instead of 2.

So a brand that is positioned to take advantage of a gap in the market, that has a brand identity exemplifying this, that communicates its key advantages well to the market and that delivers the expected quality of product or service will gain an exponential advantage through this alignment.

By analysing the elements that make up the brand, the brand owner can identify the contribution of each element to the brand, which will then enable him to rectify non-aligned elements. This gives him greater control over the brand, and greater efficiency and effectiveness by spending time and resources where they will have the best effect. By dividing this equation by the costs of the brand, the brand owner gets a clear view of the efficiency of his marketing.

The model will become clearer throughout the text.

Consistent mediocrity may be better than inconsistent brilliance. Even if I hate what it signifies (that it may be OK to be mediocre), it is true about brand management. I am not aware of any brand that has always only been brilliant. Not even Apple has. But I am aware of many brands that are mostly good or great, even if they may be mediocre at times.

 In all my years working on the Sasol Oil business, we made very many great commercials. Some were also very average. Yet, added together, they grew the brand, despite the misses. The reason is simply that one commercial is built on the previous one. We measured each one of them, and what was amazing was that consumers even liked those that were weaker. Our only logical deduction was that it was because there was a certain predisposition about Sasol commercials that made them positive – even before the viewers saw any new one.

I am sure this applied to the commercials that built the Vodacom brand, because they were all thematically linked. Some of them were decidedly weaker than others, yet collectively they created an aura of familiarity and likeability that started with "Yebo Gogo".

There was a brilliant advertising campaign for Nescafé Gold in the UK many years ago, one that used the concept of a soap opera, with a new episode every week. It was highly successful for the

brand. Two neighbours were attracted to one another, and through careful wordplay and anecdotes, they always stopped short of kissing, but people loved the repartee. Consumers like to see and hear stories about brands. It makes a brand a welcome friend in the household. I have yet to meet a client that does not want that.

Any brand can achieve short-term success based on anecdotal good luck. A great advertising campaign can do it, a great promotion can do it, a low price can do it. Yet few brands will become hugely successful based on anecdotal hits.

Many brands survive for many years based on a succession of short-term initiatives. What these brand developers do not realise is that with a slight change in emphasis and better thinking, they will be able to achieve more. And on top of it, they will actually do it for less money over time.

By creating a sustainable campaign theme in its advertising, we were actually able to spend less marketing money over the years with the Sasol Oil brand. Over time, the awareness of a given commercial grows exponentially, which means you can reduce the number of times you air it. This truly translates into savings and into building a strong brand. (I have used ongoing tracking research surveys and the ground-breaking work by Millward Brown Impact extensively for this over the years for many of my clients.)

Great brand communications campaigns work, there is little doubt about it. Similarly, great viral campaigns, like the Old Spice campaign, work.

When we launched McCarthy Call-A-Car, we knew we needed to be on television to establish the brand in those days. We made a series of three television commercials that established the brand fast.

We used well-known characters, which is often a "cheap-cop-out", but it gave us fast impact. We also used the same people in the series of three commercials. The three commercials set up the key selling points of why people should use Call-A-Car. It worked, fast. Once we created awareness, the brand had a platform we could start using. Without first creating a platform in retail, you may never reach enough people to make the brand viable across the volumes of sales it requires.

 Even though in retrospect these commercials were really not great, they got the message across and, within two years, Call-A-Car sold a large percentage of used cars and was visited by overseas dealers to learn. By carefully monitoring the audience we attracted with our television advertising, we could refine the expenditure pattern of McCarthy Call-A-Car to a point where we actually increased the profit margin per car sold without increasing the budget.

The company itself did a lot to create the infrastructure to make it work:
• liaison with dealers;
• the right sales system;
• balancing supply and demand; and

• communicating internally with their dealer network about the benefits of Call-A-Car for all dealers.

It reinforced my perception that great marketing takes an integrated effort; it cannot be delegated to the marketing department or, even worse, the agency.

The key is to retain elements of cosistency but introduce new innovative ideas regularly. This is a fine balance and few brands do this well. When we deal with brand core values later in this book, I will give pointers on how to do this.

Most companies have access to internal information and can use it to manage their brands better – they just do not use it. Anything we do in marketing has an outcome. It is whether we learn from it that matters.

I have seen many similar examples. When you know what to do, things get simple. The better you know a brand, the easier it gets for the brand owner and for consumers. For years, Corolla lagged behind Golf in brand and advertising awareness, something that concerned Toyota and me as an agency person. We changed this almost overnight by launching a series of commercials that were thematically linked, because we showed the same character in a few typical situations.

Today, Toyota practices the same principle by using a dog that speaks. Even though some people may now be bored with it, the upside for the brand is probably still greater than the downside. It is not easy to decide when to stop and start something new, but it certainly is better to have consistency than to change every time.

Stories work in marketing, as they do in life.

We had the privilege to work for Battery Centre and needed to achieve great results with a low budget. Anyone can do well with a large budget, you have to be pretty dumb not to. A small budget challenges you.

We thought the team of Willie Esterhuizen and Lizz Meiring would be excellent to tell the Battery Centre story because they were by then well established through a number of television series in which they acted together. So we made three commercials for R30 000 (all inclusive), a very modest expenditure at a time when the average television commercial cost more than R750 000 to make.

The ads were arguably not great, but because they told a story and used well-known characters who had a heritage of their own, Battery Centre became a household name fast.

So how do you ensure that your brand management is systematic yet still dynamic and engaging? How do you mix analysis with creativity in a manner that consistently creates brand value? How do all the elements hang together – and how can you relate them?

My recipe works, even if you are a bad chef

On page 17 I outline the way I look at brands diagrammatically. This is the way I manage brands and how I believe the factors that make up a brand fit together. I will outline this model step by step, and it will become increasingly clear as we progress.

A brand is a complex entity in which a number of critical elements come together to make the brand work. Understanding this dynamic helps us to launch and manage brands, and it also helps us to understand when things go wrong with our brands. Although these factors work together as a whole, each one of them also has to adhere to certain characteristics.

Let me explain these basic elements of the model in Diagram 1.

DIAGRAM 1

MARKET, INDUSTRY & COMPETITIVE FACTORS

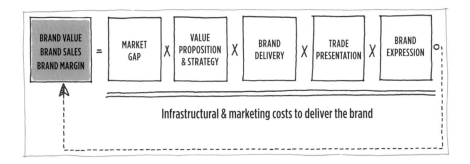

First, the environment. Any brand exists in an environment that provides it with opportunities to grow and also places restrictions on it. In this context, the brand satisfies the needs of selected segments of the market. The brand sits in the place where these elements overlap with the capabilities of the company. These are the macro factors, of which we distinguish the following categories:

- Market determinants such as the economy, technology, socio-politics, population number and growth rate, and legislation;
- The competitive environment;
- The industry rules of the game;
- The needs and wants of consumers; and
- The ability of the brand owner to exploit opportunities.

Second, the process. In this environment, brand value can be created, built and maintained in a process consisting of the following key micro factors that must be managed and aligned:

- The market opportunity;
- The brand value proposition and

how that translates into the marketing and brand strategy;
- The name and identity of the brand;
- The marketing communications of the brand;
- The delivery of the brand (i.e. its quality and service); and
- The distribution of the brand (where it can be bought and how impactful it is there).

The above is matched to our own capabilities as a company and what it costs us to grow and maintain the brand.

Alignment

The success of a brand depends on the alignment of all these elements, while with every single step that we take, we need to do the best job we can.

The alignment of elements can create an exponential benefit. The more the process within the environment is aligned to the brand objectives and positioning, the greater the value created will be and the higher the potential profit margin (above the average for the category). Eventually this will have the consequence of greater efficiency and effectiveness of brand management.

In addition, given that these factors are aligned, the greater the likelihood will be that the entire company and its resources are attuned to creating brand value for consumers. It will even beg the question why company functions exist that do not directly add to the creation of brand value.

In Diagram 2, I outline typical questions you need to ask about the brand or customer profitability.

DIAGRAM 2

Business objectives: Typical questions that must translate into strategic and tactical questions about consumer retention, value growth, acquisition and churn.

Customer profit margin trends:
- How do they compare with industry trends?
- Are there different trends in related industries that satisfy the same consumer needs? If so, why?

Market share in numbers and value:
- What is the trend?
- Why is it so?

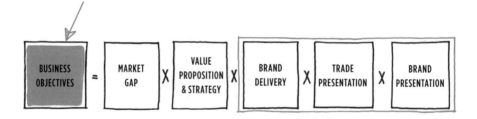

Once we have reviewed our brand, we will be able to identify its strengths and weaknesses (see Diagram 3). This helps us to know what needs to change to increase the impact and value of our brand. We can thus apply a "weight" to every aspect of our brand (average, strong = +2, or weak = -1). Whilst some of this is subjective, or by management agreement, you can make it as rigorous as possible with hard internal and research data. Much of the information required exists in most companies. Even if you use it fairly superficially as a guideline only, it can assist you to know where to focus.

DIAGRAM 3

A successful brand is a function of coordinated activities in a number of areas. The factors combine in an "equation". They incrementally build on each other or detract from each other.

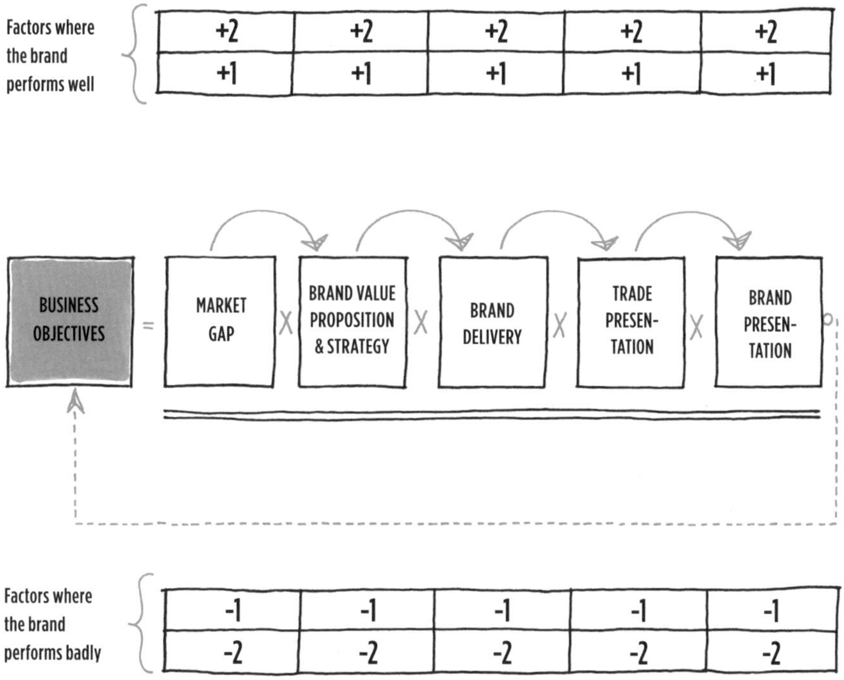

Factors where the brand performs well				
+2	+2	+2	+2	+2
+1	+1	+1	+1	+1

$$\text{BUSINESS OBJECTIVES} = \text{MARKET GAP} \times \text{BRAND VALUE PROPOSITION \& STRATEGY} \times \text{BRAND DELIVERY} \times \text{TRADE PRESENTATION} \times \text{BRAND PRESENTATION}$$

Factors where the brand performs badly				
-1	-1	-1	-1	-1
-2	-2	-2	-2	-2

By using this graph we can assess where the gaps are in how we change our brand.

AS EXAMPLES:

- By aligning your brand elements you can see apperentially.
- If a brand focuses on the wrong market segments, with low growth rates and low profit potential, it cannot maximise its resource utilisation better than its rivals, so it will perform less well.
- If the advertising and other marketing communications do not express the brand positioning, they will undermine the brand potential and resource utilisation, as well as under-deliver in terms of growth.
- If a brand is focused on the opportunity markets and is marketed well, it will still be undermined if bad service is delivered to its existing customers. That will result in a significant amount of its marketing expenditure going to waste.
- If the brand is not available for purchase at convenient locations it undermines its potential.

DIAGRAM 4

How the different elements that make up the Apple brand align to create an impactful and efficient brand. Apple aligns its product design, functionality, with packaging that conveys expectation and surprise, with advertising that has a certain attitude, and with store displays and staff that enhance the uniqueness of the brand experience. Conceptually, the brand hangs together.

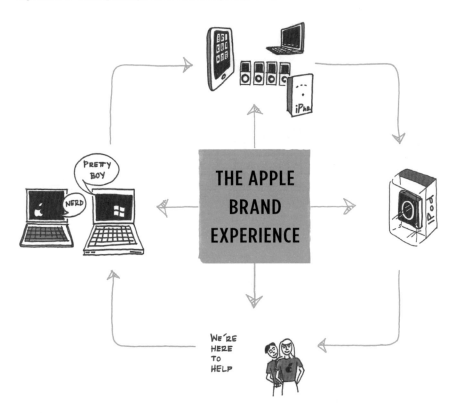

In the next chapter I shall explain the macro factors in more depth.

THREE

MACRO FACTORS

WE NEED TO CONSIDER

- All competitors start on an equal footing

- Great brands grow even in an economic downturn

- Many guess; few know for a fact

- Companies conduct a lot of market research on consumers, but in reality the consumer is not at the centre of most large companies

- A brand owner is often unrealistic about whether it has what it takes to be an industry leader

- You need to go beyond benchmarking – you need to create a competitive advantage

A brand exists in an external macro environment. There are macro factors that determine the market opportunity and the restrictions on it. As businesspeople, we need to understand the macro circumstances within which we operate, to leverage them in the best possible way.

All competitors in a given product or service category start this race on an equal footing. The one that is best able to leverage the environmental opportunities will succeed in creating above-average brand value.

DIAGRAM 5

The market & competitive opportunity: typical questions

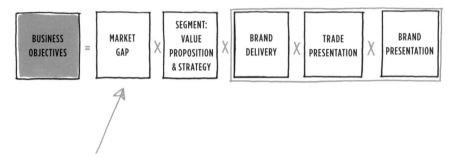

- Consider market size, growth, penetration rate.
     Is there a market opportunity left?
- Consider market segments and proliferation. Consider market needs and occupied positions.
     Is there a market opportunity left?
- What is required to either consolidate (retain), grow or exit?
- Can the brand we have do that? if not, what else can?
- Consider market dynamics (e.g. innovation, new entrants & profitability rates).
     Does the opportunity lie "within"? If so, where?
     Does the opportunity lie "outside"? If so, where?
- Consider drivers and inhibitors of growth.
- What is the trend and likely trend?

The market determinants

This category consists of factors, such as economic growth, that will determine consumers' ability to buy given goods and services, or legislation that will make it easy or difficult for consumers to operate in a given environment. It will determine the number of consumers that make up what is called the addressable market, therefore the number of people able and willing to spend money on the product or service.

Generally, at least five factors are reviewed: the economic environment; the socio-political environment; the population and its demographic trends; the technological environment; and the legislative environment.

The factors that constitute the market environment will either drive or inhibit the growth of the market a brand is in. Generally, business thrives in a market environment where consumers are confident, able and willing to spend money. If the market environment is not conducive to consumer spending, we need to make sure that our brand has a greater-than-average chance to succeed. Great brands grow even in an economic downturn.

Just by reviewing the impact of economic turmoil on consumer confidence and spending patterns, one can see how important this factor is. When an economy is in decline, people not only have less money to spend, they have less inclination to spend it.

Even in such circumstances, some brands succeed better than others. But, in general, the sentiment of a given market will impact most brands to a greater or a lesser extent.

A given brand cannot control these factors but it may be able to influence some of them. The important thing for a brand is not to rely on market factors to determine its fate. It needs to understand these factors so well that it will succeed despite these. The best brands do see declines in their fortunes when economies decline but they generally decline far less than other brands.

It seems the practice that works best for companies is to use Delphi types of workshops, where the senior executives, assisted by specialist resources as required, will debate the key market determinants for their industry, rate their importance to determine which are most likely to impact them, and then plan how to respond to these to the company's advantage.

My view is that you should focus on the three or four issues that really drive and constrain market potential, and then quantify and manage these. There is little point in laundry lists of factors and statistics that have little or no impact on the company.

If the fate of our company is entirely exposed to the ebbs and flows of external factors, we are simply not managing it properly. Then computers can do our jobs as managers better.

Competitive and industry-specific factors

Very few companies or brands are lucky enough to have the market opportunities to themselves. They mostly compete with other brands, some with greater and others with fewer resources. It is important to know what factors within the competitive environment will make your brand succeed. In an article in the *Harvard Business Review* of October 2011, the CEO of Heinz, Bill Johnson, states that four factors determine emerging-market success:

- Applicability – the product addresses the needs of local consumers;
- Availability – the product is available where consumers need it;
- Affordability – the product is available in the size and format that enables consumers to buy it within limited means; and
- Affinity – creating a desirable brand consumers love.

What factors will make your company succeed over others? How do you best leverage the value you create for consumers with the resources you have access to? How do you build greater value than your competitors with the same or fewer resources? Unless you know, you can easily spend money in the wrong places, or you will be unable to say with certainty whether you are doing the right things.

Alan Knott-Craig was the visionary founding CEO of Vodacom in South Africa, which became the leading telecommunications company. His vision was clear from the beginning. He knew which factors he had to excel at to create a winning company:
- have the best network, with the best coverage and capacity;
- have the best airtime sales network; and
- have the strongest brand.

Defining its competitive imperatives is vital for a successful company. No investor wants to invest in, or staff member wants to work for, a company that is unclear about what will make it outperform its peers.

Although competitors should never determine your strategy, you need to be aware of what they do and in which ways they are better or worse than you. I am always fascinated by how many companies do not really know where they are ahead of or behind competitors. Many guess; few know for a fact.

The competitive environment includes all brands that deliver the same, or a similar, value proposition to consumers. During a time of increasing industry convergence, they are no longer confined to the companies we would traditionally have defined as competitors. The famous strategist Gary Hamel states that 90% of what happens in most industries today happens outside the traditional ambit of competitors.

Consumers often use a combination of brands to satisfy a given problem, without regard for clear boundaries. Nowhere is that more true today than in the ways consumers use telecommunications, internet service providers, media and information technology suppliers.

The competitive opportunity provides the industry benchmarks against which any company must measure itself. It must be at least as good as the industry norm to succeed. Alternatively, its price must compensate for a lower level of customer satisfaction (for example, consumers know that by paying less for low-cost airlines, they will sacrifice some of the benefits associated with traditional airlines).

A company needs to fully understand its competitors to enable it to leverage its market opportunities better than rival brands.

Consumer needs

It remains a fundamental truth that satisfying customer needs better than competitors makes a business successful. If consumers are what marketing is all about, we need to live that principle in how the consumer permeates all we do. Yet, although many companies conduct a lot of market research to understand their consumers and their needs, in reality the consumer is not at the centre of most large companies.

Satisfying consumer needs takes a deep commitment from a business. It needs to align its resources to truly deliver what customers expect.

The multiplier effect of exceptional quality of product or service aimed at customers is enormous and it creates a wave of goodwill. I have yet to find a customer-obsessed company that does not succeed.

In the middle nineties, the Tesco retail chain in the UK started by first and foremost fixing the basics of its business: the right merchandise, in a pleasant shopping environment and with trained staff able to deliver the service people expect. Over the years, it built onto this. Today, the re-emergence of Tesco is a global case study.

Some years ago, when Christo Davel started 20twenty, the first online bank in South Africa, I was sceptical that he could offer the exceptional service he promised. Yet he did that, and customers became advocates for the brand overnight. The same was true of René Otto when he started Outsurance. He aligned the IT systems, call centres, people training and structures to deliver a superior service.

As brand owners we do not create needs. We identify them and then respond to them as we choose. The way we serve customers' needs has to go way beyond simply asking them what they need. Great brands are built because companies listen to consumers and observe them, and then interpret what they need in the light of what their own insights and technology enable them to do.

Consumers are not going to say they need an iPad, but they are going to respond when one is delivered because the iPad is a response to a host of underlying needs. On top of that, these needs are then exploited by great packaging, by the design and look and feel of the products.

You may respond to the needs and wants of the whole market if you are a large company or a first-mover, or you may respond to one or more segments of the market where your company is able to satisfy customer needs better than other companies.

The value proposition you are able to offer will also determine that. If it addresses the needs of a wide group of people, a mass approach is right. If it satisfies the needs of only a given segment, a focused approach is right. Much of this decision is made on the basis of the capabilities and resources of the company, not only in marketing but in all other areas of the business.

This is one area where I see most companies fail. They do not sharp-shoot, they seem to target everyone, often losing focus and wasting resources. Identify the right targets that will enable growth at the desired profit margin, and go for it in a logical and systematic manner.

 Breaking the market up in smaller groups, each with similar needs, is called market segmentation. All it involves, at its core, is to group people together who have more or less the same needs.

While there are many academic debates about the best approach to segmentation, mine is quite simple. We need to segment the market in a way that enables us to market according to the needs of consumers – in a way that makes it possible for us to measure progress against the chosen segments.

If segments become too theoretical, it is very difficult to use them to market or to measure. When you cannot market to them or measure them, the segments are theoretical and of little use to a company. Most segmentation projects suffer from this problem.

Segments are hardly ever entirely mutually exclusive. If a segment is stated as male, it does not mean there are no females in the segment. It simply means most are male – but this majority may be small (for example, 55/45).

I have found the following parameters work best when we segment:
- Make sure you define your market as consumers see it, not as you see it. This will include peripheral need areas that related brands will satisfy (for example, banks are only one option for investments).
- Use the language consumers use in your category, not the technical language you use. Qualitative research is good in helping you to identify this.
- Start with usage and make sure you can get back to measuring usage after you have implemented the segmentation. Usage is often the only measurable sales we have in a company.
- Overlay the needs of consumers onto this.

- Overlay the lifestyle, attitudes, aspirations and beliefs that determine the needs people have.
- Overlay the demographics of the market that make it possible for us to identify these consumers when we want to market to them. This is the only way to compare research results with demographic data from other surveys (for example, media usage patterns).
- Overlay the brand awareness and perceptions of our own and competitive brands. This enables us to manage the health of our brand within the segments of importance to us.
- Some companies overlay customer satisfaction levels of their own and competitive brands. This is useful as it gives us a far better understanding of the odds when expanding.

Most segmentation questionnaires are too long. In my experience, the factors that are really important are often fewer, not more. By using multi-variate statistics, one can sort the attributes generated through upfront research to identify those that really matter.

In most instances, a number of questions get exactly the same response from consumers. We must remember that they do not understand the nuances as we do. To use a simple example: to telecommunications companies, "coverage" may mean geographical coverage and call quality (for example, not dropping calls because of network load). Consumers often do not discriminate between the two.

Also remember that any company that does segmentation in the same industry will obtain very much the same results. It is not the fact that you do segmentation – it is how it is interpreted and used that matters. I have seen companies that do fairly rudimentary segmentation and use it well.

Competitive advantage is when we leverage segmentation in ways unique to our company and brands. If we simply use the segments as they are identified, we will do no more and no less than any competitor with similar segmentation results. Yet, many companies still look at segmentation as an end in itself.

The company's capabilities

The last factor that I include in the list of macro factors is the ability of the brand owner to take up these market opportunities. This includes the core capabilities and competitive advantage of the brand owner.

Does your company have what it takes to be the leader in your industry? This is important because in my experience often companies do not consider these or are very unrealistic about them. If your company does not have the right infrastructure, systems, processes and trained staff, you cannot deliver better service than your peers. Be honest about what you are good at and make sure that you put the programmes in place that will enable you to offer a given value proposition to a customer. It may be useful to apply a 360 degree review of your company capabilities, in which investors and analysts, the media, management, staff, suppliers, clients and even influencers

in society are used to review your actual level of competence. I have yet to see the company that will not gain from a fair assessment of its own abilities. You will have to be open to hearing negative things though, which is not something most CEO's like.

The outcomes of such reviews may be simple, like when Tesco returned to basics, or it may be complex, like Apple offering products with a superior design. Whatever you decide, make sure you can deliver it. It is better to be honest about your shortfalls than to infuriate customers because you fail to deliver.

In most industries, there are parameters most companies need to adhere to. We need to know these. They are the rules of the game. I always look at two sets. One is the basics we need to have to be able to operate, like access to aircraft, landing slots and staff to be able to run an airline. The other set is what sets us apart from competitors and will make us do better than them, all else being equal. These are the differentiators.

Well-regarded management consultant Tony Manning says that unless you change the design of what you do, you cannot change the outcome. This is a simple truth. Strange how many times I have seen companies miss this point.

The process of benchmarking can be useful in assessing the ability of a company to match best practice in its own industry. Benchmarking is less useful when we believe that is all we need to do in a company – that we will succeed by simply being like everyone else. A company needs more.

Beyond benchmarking the best, we still need to offer a competitive advantage. Since only one company can be the largest in any industry, most will not only have to match best practice but also give consumers a compelling point of difference. If a company does not do that, it becomes a me-too brand, which results in lower profit margins and – in most cases – less loyal consumers.

FOUR

CREATING BRAND VALUE

- Only the brand owner can define what he wants the brand to achieve: how he will define its "value"

- Despite ideological debates about the future viability of capitalism, a business still needs to create more wealth than it consumes. Unless it does that, it cannot create jobs, pay tax or contribute to society

- Reciprocity between brand and society is the norm today

- A brand owner needs to know whether his brand is growing, and he needs to know how and why

- Define your brand objectives well and remain on top of progress. Understand "early warning signals"

- Understanding your customer gains and losses are very powerful measurements. You need to know this

I n this chapter we will focus on the concept of brand value.

What is the value of the brand to the brand owner? This is the asset value of the brand (if it were to be sold) as well as the consistent source of revenue and the profit margin it provides.

Traditionally, the definition of brand success was very simply based on return on shareholder equity. Other stakeholders were secondary to investors. In this equation, it is fair to assume that the more profitable a brand, the more successful it is. If return on capital  employed is the only real measure of success, it is logical that investors will invest where they can make the most money.

Over time, this measure has been debated and adapted as other interest groups and global issues started impacting on the way in which companies operate. This includes the rights of staff; the transparency forced on companies by legislation and the media; and community and environmental issues.

So return on shareholder equity is no longer the only issue to be considered. Yet it remains the reason why capital will be available for a company to operate, even though other factors now make the management of a company more complex. These additional fac- tors can now erode shareholder value as well as the longevity of a company. In this changing world, the yardstick of business success is what the investors, directors and executive management of the company regard as the criterion for their business. The investors that provide the capital have to evaluate how it will create a sustainable business, and the factors that are significant for doing so.

Jack Welch, iconic past CEO of GE, in a clip from his MBA series, states that the objective of any management is to win. If it does not win, it does not have any money to pay staff, to invest back into society, or to mentor and train people. If a business does badly, it not only disappoints its shareholders, it is also incapable of investing in its staff and society.

The concept of brand value encapsulates whatever makes up the measure of brand success that is applied by a brand owner. In most instances, its defining measure of success will remain return to shareholders, but it will have to do this in a more reciprocal context to other stakeholders than before.

A company can survive in the long term only if it can generate more cash than it uses. Sometimes a government or philanthrope invests regardless of a company's ability to make money, but even then the money comes from somewhere else in the first place.

Malcolm McDonald from the Cranfield School of Business believes marketing has only two objectives. These are, first, to retain and grow the sales from existing customers and, second, to attract new customers. These two objectives encapsulate the contribution that marketing can make to a company. The impact of these factors on brand value

is arguably more important than the contribution of any other factors, except for sales themselves.

To assess the value of the brand, we need to ask the following types of questions about its current strength:

- Am I growing customers faster than my competitors? If not, why not?
- Am I retaining or losing customers? If I am losing customers, why? What profile of customers am I losing? Are they the kind I can afford to lose?
- Am I growing the business I get from existing customers?
- Am I growing in the market segments where the growth potential is best?
- How strongly is my brand positioned for future revenue and profit growth?
- How does my brand compare with the same or related consumer need categories in achieving new revenue or margin growth?
- Can my brand extend into new markets and sources of revenue?
- What is the asset value of my brand – and is it growing?
- What market or competitive changes are likely to impact the future value or profitability of my brand?
- What entrants into my current or related market are achieving high levels of growth or profitability?
- Am I growing new sources of revenue in products or services?

These questions point to the performance factors that will create brand value. If all these factors are taken into account, the brand is likely to succeed.

Furthermore, if these factors are all aligned, the gain for the brand will be exponential. If any of these factors are not aligned, the equation will be undermined and the result will be a drop in the value of the brand. This drop will also be exponential.

Five factors determine for how long a given brand will remain profitable:

1. The user growth rate for the product or service category. The higher the growth rate, the more likely it is that a certain level of profitability can be sustained; the lower, the more likely that price competition will start eroding profit margins.
2. The ability of the brand and the brand team to stimulate its customers through regular innovation and customer intimacy.
3. The level of brand innovation in the category. Generally, higher levels of innovation in an industry will build greater value for all the players, yet the most innovative brands will benefit most.
4. The degree to which the brand balances the interests of all important stakeholders, such as staff and communities.
5. The degree to which the brand is able to satisfy consumer needs at a lower cost than competitors can.

When a brand experiences a problem, you need to ask the following types of questions:
- Is there a need in the marketplace for my brand? Sometimes there may be a need, but it may be in a very small portion of the market.
- What factors drive the market size and sales for my brand?
- Is my brand offering anything different from my main competitors?
- Is my brand positioned in the right area? Even when there is a great need, we do not always connect the consumer need with the positioning, so we confuse customers. We can even drop the price to make them buy, like with many of the Apple iPad's competitors. Almost any product has a level of price at which people will buy it.
- Are my target-market consumers aware of my brand? Is this spontaneous or prompted? If consumers are not aware, they cannot buy. Yet, we can prompt them at point of sale with great signage, packaging, merchandising or displays.
- Are they aware of my marketing? If so, what are they saying about my brand? In most large categories, one or two brands will dominate perception, which means smaller brands need to work hard at differentiating themselves.
- Are the messages about my brand those that I need to communicate to get my target-market consumers to try out the brand? If one message does not work, try another. Surely you do not tell your friends the same joke over and over again? Either they laugh the first time, or they do not.
- Am I using the right media to convey these messages of my brand? This is complex. Am I reaching the right people often enough, in accordance with their purchasing and decision-making cycles?

- Are the users of my brand satisfied with the brand? If not, why not? What can I do about it? If they are satisfied, are they advocates for my brand? Am I increasing their usage of my brand? If not, why not? How do I compare with other brands in my category?
- How does this differ by market segment? Am I stronger in some than in others? If so, why? How does that compare with my brand awareness and perceptions?
- Are my consumers starting to use replacement products and services? Why?
- Is my number of customers growing or shrinking? Is the value of my share growing or shrinking? If the value is in decline, is this because I give excessive discounts or because consumers think less of my brand?
- Do I know how my brand is performing in brand awareness, advertising awareness, sales volumes and value, market share, and profit relative to competitors?
- Is my brand in stock where and when people want to buy it?
- Does the rate of purchasing in the category increase or decrease and how does that compare with my brand?
- Are there emerging trends that impact my growth? In what way? What can I do about it?

These questions will enable brand owners to manage their brands in a way that will maximise their potential.

FIVE

SEARCHING FOR
THE BRAND GAP

- Great product or service ideas still drive business! They still create greater brand value than most other things

- Many brand ideas are parity – they offer nothing new or different. This means their results will be parity, at best

- Many marketers believe their brand will work despite having no significant benefit that differentiates it from competitors

- Simple ideas work!

- Product or service ideas have to be supported by aligning company infrastructure – every activity of a company needs to be evaluated to determine to how it creates value for customers in delivering the brand idea

When Akio Morita of Sony saw joggers in Tokyo run with transistor radios on their shoulders, he created the Sony Walkman in response. He identified that joggers needed something to lighten their boredom, something easy and convenient to carry with them.

He identified how he could combine the capabilities of his company with the needs of consumers. He had found and filled a brand gap. His response created a revolutionary product that went way beyond satisfying the needs of joggers.

A brand gap is simply the space or opportunity within the needs of my chosen consumers that I decide to fill with my product or service. It is a response to the questions of what consumers need, and why – and when, how and where they will use it.

More formally, a brand gap or market opportunity can be defined as a gap where the market trends, consumer needs, competitive environment and company capabilities meet. And any new market opportunity will require the alignment of company resources to take advantage of it.

In my experience, marketers do not consider, first, if there still is an opportunity for a new brand, and second, if they can offer a brand that is different enough to gain sufficient market share to be a viable player.

 Identifying a brand gap is one of the greatest challenges a marketer faces. Reading the gap correctly takes consumer insight, competitive insight, marketing insight, industry insight and company insight.

To some extent, consumer research can indicate gaps in the market not currently filled by competitors.

Often, the best competitive advantage does not lie in simply offering another brand in a heavily contested space but by looking at what is now called a blue ocean strategy (Kim & Mauborgne), which entails a lateral approach to the market instead of the traditional approach.

The ability of the company to deliver

Once the gap has been assessed, we have to evaluate the degree to which the company can deliver on the identified gap. This is done by a situational analysis, in which the company assesses its own strengths and weaknesses. This gives it a realistic base to work from. The best way to do this is to compare the market gap with the capabilities of the company that wants to take advantage of it. This needs to be done objectively. We need to be clear about what the company is not capable of and what it is capable of. It may mean that remedial steps have to be taken to address some of the possible weaknesses in order to take advantage of a market opportunity.

It is my concern that many brand owners unrealistically over-value their own ability to deliver to consumers. For example, many companies believe they can offer consumers better service, even if they have no substantive reason for saying so, whether in systems or people. In such instances, it is likely that the advantage gained by an unrealistic claim will be short-lived.

I learnt this lesson early on in my days in marketing. When I was running the advertising for Volkskasbank in my late twenties, we launched a highly impactful campaign called Service Excellence in Banking. It attracted large numbers of customers of the right profile. Yet, these customers were demanding and expected the best – their reason for switching to us. I failed to realise at the time that we simply did not have the trained people and information systems to offer these customers superior service. As soon as we attracted them, many defected again.

When we launched McCarthy Call-A-Car in my days at my own agency, I learnt another key lesson. Soon after launch, we experienced stock shortages of certain makes of vehicles – while many dealers had stock. When we investigated, we discovered that many dealers did not want to become part of the system of pooling their stock as they thought as a smaller dealer they had less chance to sell. We had to work hard to break down this myth.

It is surprising how often this kind of problem occurs in business. The Dis-Chem pharmacy chain has a system that tracks standing prescriptions and then informs you by phone when your new prescription is ready for collection. This is a great service. But twice I have received a call and arrived to find my prescription was not ready because the pharmacy was out of stock. Clearly, no one thought to check on the availability of stock before making the call.

This is an example of a great "added-value" benefit that could have been a competitive advantage but was not thought through by the company.

The above examples illustrate the fact that marketing is never the task of one person or one department. The entire company and its infrastructure need to align behind the value proposition made to the customer.

Some useful questions to ask in attempting to find and fill a gap:

- What growth and profit opportunities are there in terms of market segments and value propositions?
- How large or profitable are these opportunities?
- What new spaces can be created that my brand can dominate?
- How far can my brand stretch?
- If a new growth opportunity is strong enough, how can I create a brand to play there?
- What are the chances that I can redefine the competitive landscape entirely with a new brand?

The brand idea – four pointers

On the basis of the analysis above, the brand owner now has a realistic assessment of what can be offered to the consumer.

The brand idea is the value proposition, or the offer the brand makes, to its consumers. In the instance of Ryanair, it is cheap flights to desirable destinations.

Here are four pointers for brand ideas to consider:

First, brand ideas should address consumer needs – and be simple and easy for consumers to relate to and understand.

This is one of the most problematical issues in marketing. We as businesspeople and marketers understand our business so well, we assume others do too. The fact is that consumers do not – not even highly sophisticated businesspeople. It is not their business. Hence it is up to us to make sure our consumers understand what we are trying to sell them.

Simplicity in marketing is a very important issue that is mostly neglected. We usually complicate what we offer consumers, and marketers are more likely to add layers of complexity to value propositions and campaigns than they are likely to simplify them.

  I have experience of brand managers re-writing advertising copy so that it makes sense to them, adding lists of consumer benefits. Most consumers do not read copy in such detail and will either not be interested in, or understand, lists of brand benefits. Keep it simple and sell the consumer a single-value proposition: simple, relevant and to the point.

"If a product's use is apparent, simple and clear, it will stand out from all those that compete for our attention," James Utterback states in *Design-Inspired Innovation*. Good brand and product design is often about reducing, not adding, complexity.

When consumers can immediately understand how a product fits into their lives, how it can benefit them and how they can use it, it is the fastest way to market. Ideas that are easy to understand find traction fast in a universe that is over-extended with offers to consumers, messages to consumers and general information overload. The Sony Walkman offered consumers something very simple: a small, compact and portable way to transport their favourite music, with the additional benefit of listening to it on headphones in private. This simple idea had market impact fast. This was replicated years later by MP3 players – in particular, the iPod.

Strong ideas are simple ideas. In *Brand Simple*, the managing director of Landor Associates, Allen Adamson, sees this as a vital determinant of the success of most highly valuable brands. He cites Dawn detergent, with its simple idea: Dawn takes grease out of your way. We know that the awareness levels of advertising are declining in most developed markets. People are simply less and less likely to hear and see the claims a brand makes, even if it spends a considerable amount of money to do so. With this trend, getting a complex message across is very difficult. In my experience, it hardly ever happens unless a company spends vast amounts of money.

Adamson sees a brand idea as being unique and simple to grasp. He also cites how this was easy in the early days of marketing when Ivory was soap, Hershey's was chocolate, and Maxwell House was coffee (at the time "deep, rich flavour" was enough). Today, this is much more difficult as the number of brands in any category is so large. We should never assume that consumers are that interested in what we do. They want to be told, in an instant, why our brand will offer them superior benefits. Our brand needs an elevator statement, to state the benefits it offers in less than 30 seconds. Although this is a challenge to achieve, it will also be great to help staff focus on what is really important.

Second, we are moving from product and service brands to idea or concept brands.

Brands were historically tied to industries. Banks compete in the banking sector, airlines in the airline sector.

Brands defined particular products, such as a Hoover being the term used for vacuum cleaners, even for those that do not bear the Hoover label. Colgate was used for toothpaste. In these instances, the brand name has become generic, taking on the meaning of the category.

 When a business's definition of industry is too narrow, that business will face a decline as soon as new technology replaces its offering. Many industries have declined because of this:

- The computer industry did not notice that management consultants entered their arena, thereby reducing them to sellers of hardware at low prices.
- The software industry was not con-

scious enough of the ways that open systems, applications and cloud computing were becoming a major competitive threat.

- The telecommunications industry still believed that they were carriers of voice and data only, despite Skype and Google satellites possibly threatening them as carriers.
- Banks saw themselves as the only deposit takers.
- Bookshops were not conscious enough of the potential and impact of online bookstores such as Amazon.com, which was made even more opportune by the development of Kindle and iPads.
- Some types of mining were not conscious enough of new technology replacing some natural resources over time.
- Preventative drugs replaced traditional drugs and even medical intervention, as in dentistry.

There are hardly any industries that are not changing dramatically. In many of these instances, the emerging competitors are from outside traditional industries. Consumers started buying bank products from retailers, music from Apple, financial services from Virgin and fuel from Tesco.

Some brands have been able to straddle their product or service categories with ease, while many have been unable to do so. I call the kinds of brands that can do this easily "concept brands". Concept brands are not tied to a given product or service category. They can straddle many categories, often because they have very strong philosophical brand

perceptions that set them apart. A very good example of a concept brand is Apple, which has been able to straddle several product categories successfully: personal computers, MP3 music and video players, phones, books and music stores. Apple was able to do this because the brand attained emotional significance beyond its product category definition. Apple stands for products that are uniquely designed in appearance and functionality – and are fun and easy to use. This means the Apple brand can be extended into many categories where its uniqueness can upset the existing brand paradigm.

Using its core competence – producing crystals of very high quality – Swarovski has been able to extend from being a manufacturer of small crystal ornaments with a limited market reach into many product categories such as fashion accessories, furniture, lighting, binoculars, camera lenses, jewellery, watches, toys, handbags, toilet seats, headphones, interior decorating, flash disks and mobile phone covers, with more being added by the day.

Some brands have successfully adapted their very descriptive names to attain a wider meaning: a name like GE is more used today than General Electric. Kentucky Fried Chicken changed its name to KFC, thereby under-playing the significance of fried chicken in a health-conscious world. Likewise, Apple adapted its name from Apple Computer to Apple Incorporated.

It is not always a given that concept brands are better than product brands. Where a given brand so clearly dominates a category, it may be unwise to potentially undermine its single-mindedness and simplicity.

Third, if you are not the first mover in a new category, the largest or the cheapest, your brand idea needs to be differentiated.

One of the most annoying things I encounter in marketing is that many marketers believe their brand will work despite having no significant benefit that differentiates it from competitors. In many instances, marketers do not even know why their brand is working – or more importantly, not working.

Me-too brands are one of the most annoying issues in marketing, eroding the value of marketing in an organisation and signifying a lack of insight, thinking and creativity in a marketing department. If a marketer does not add differentiated value to a brand, we must question what the marketing department does. Surely, marketing needs to create the value that enables the brand to sell at a higher margin than its competitors.

Neumeier states: "Only one competitor can be the cheapest – the others have to use branding." And, according to Theodore Levitt in *The Marketing Imagination*, "meaningful distinction" is vitally important in an era of "crowded markets and global competition".

I was told by a friend who did work for one of the largest banks in South Africa that when he asked the marketing department in a meeting one day how their bank was positioned (after they had just spent millions of rands on a new campaign), no one could give him a straight answer without anecdotal and generic statements.

This is sad, but also criminal. How can you do your job as a marketer – and all pull in the same direction – if you do not know that? More importantly, how can a marketing department be the flag carrier for the consumer to all other departments in the bank if it does not know that? If it has no clarity, who will have?

Adamson believes that the most important decision a brand can make is in how it is differentiated. He uses the model developed by the Y&R communications agency, which cites the following brand pillars:

- Differentiation (what makes a brand unique). This is the most important pillar for a brand. Adamson states that strong brands have high levels of differentiation.
- Relevance (how important the differentiation or uniqueness is). When a brand is relevant but not differentiated, it is becoming a commodity.
- Esteem (how well regarded the brand is). When a brand has a higher level of esteem than the level of knowledge consumers have about it, it can convince more people to buy it. An example is the designer Bang & Olufsen sound system.
- Brand knowledge (how well consumers know and understand the brand).

Fourth, product or service design is an increasingly important determinant of differentiation.

Steve Jobs of Apple famously said design is not only what a product looks like, it is also how it works. Design can be seen as the entire presentation of the value proposition of the brand to the consumer, which will include its tangible and intangible elements.

In the instance of Apple, its cult following, and the excitement its products create in the marketplace and among consumers are as much part of the brand design as its features and functional benefits. One can even argue some of the historic appeal of Apple in the graphic design industry was that the products blurred the line between work and play. The user interface became rewarding in its own right.

Utterback states that design-inspired products will be more profitable and enduring.

A US survey by Kelton Research found that among consumers who saw a new product they just had to have, 70% said it was because of a unique design. Among fast-growing companies in the UK, The Design Council found that 47% ranked design first of all critical success factors for their companies (Neumeier).

Alan Lafley, the CEO of Proctor & Gamble, is attempting to make design an integral part of the company DNA. Quoted in Utterback, he states: "I think it is value that rules the world. There is... evidence across many categories that consumers will pay more for a bet

There are reasons why strong brands are strong. McDonald's was not the first drive-in burger restaurant in California, yet it was the first to create a standardised way of operating by applying factory production-line thinking to the way it prepared and served its burgers. It had a limited menu, standardised side orders, added service windows for customers to order and pick up their food, and it invested in milkshake machines that could produce five shakes at once.

The McDonald brothers called their system the Speedy Service System. This system was perfected over time, building up a unique competence that forms the foundation of the McDonald's business to this day. The processes are clear, precise and standardised. They have created a set of rules about how long to cook a burger, how to hire people, how to choose locations, how to manage stores and how to franchise stores (Roger Martin, *The Design of Business*).

The result is a set of business processes that are entirely "codified", as Martin calls it. Nothing is left to chance. For the consumers, it means that, wherever they are, they will experience the same taste and they will pay very much the same price.

Today, most global companies emulate these principles, from KFC to Starbucks to Ikea to The Four Seasons.

SIX

BRAND STRATEGY
AND POSITIONING

- Business strategy must at some point translate into brand strategy and positioning

- The most successful companies have defining value systems that permeate all they do

- Most brand strategies say nothing at all – it is just words and more words

- If people read your strategy, will they understand your brand so well that they will be able to encapsulate who you are in five words?

- Establishing a good strategy is the most intellectually challenging thing a company can do, to quote Professor Gary Hamel

- A clear brand strategy is a vital guiding principle for all aspects of your business

- Simplify/reduce = a few words drive brand ideals, consumers and staff

Once we have clarity about the brand opportunity and the brand idea, we need to decide how to position the brand. This entails the single impression we want to leave with people about the brand: what sets it apart from other brands and gives the consumer a compelling reason to buy it.

I will explain it in the context of brand strategy. A brand strategy is a very important document and must be a blueprint for the brand, one that all stakeholders must be able to relate to, understand and support.

The brand strategy must be interpreted by all departments in a company to align their activities to the philosophy behind the brand. The same applies to key suppliers of the company. If this is not done, a strategy document is just a piece of paper.

I use my own way to generate brand strategies, one I find useful because it ensures that there is an internal logic in the way a brand strategy is compiled. This consists of the consecutive steps outlined below.

DIAGRAM 6

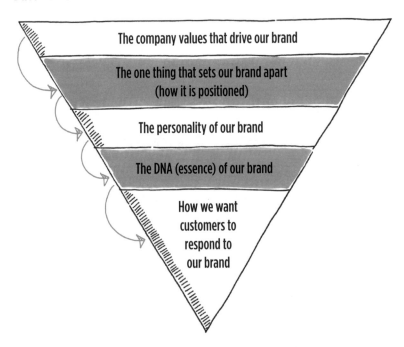

In this outline, we start compiling a brand strategy in such a way that we consecutively ask certain questions to arrive at a logical conclusion where all the elements of the strategy are aligned and mutually complementary.

Let us take a closer look at each step and at the typical questions that we have to answer about each.

The company values that drive our brand

The company values and company vision are linked. A certain vision requires a certain value system to make it work, and a certain value system will enable a certain vision. These terms need to be connected. If they are not, we are trying to be a Ferrari using Kia parts.

It is difficult for any company to perform with any brand out of sync with its very nature and the people who work for it. The most successful companies have defining value systems that permeate all they do: the people they appoint, how they operate, the kind of systems they have.

In a great article in *Forbes* of 12 September 2011, Glenn Llopis names as examples of such companies Southwest Airlines, Target, McDonald's, Apple, Nike and Facebook. He then states that not only are their philosophies simple, they have all taken on a symbolic significance that makes them more powerful than brands with less appeal. He states that these brands work because they seek to be significant.

I believe the defining values of a company are the most vital element that sets the tone for all that the company does and all the brands the company owns.

Values generic to our industry include those that are must-haves for our industry. A bank needs to be trustworthy. It is not a value that can set it apart from other brands of banks. An airline has to be safe. Without that it will not remain in business. These values are important, but they are not differentiating.

Typical questions that we have to answer to determine the company values that drive our brand:
- What values make your brand unique?
- What values would be credible for customers?
- What values can be leveraged to future advantage?
- What values are generic for most players in the industry?

The old cited example, that Disney make people "happy", is a great one that underlines how its staff believe, think and behave. Make it simple, clear, and attainable. Make it about the company. Ensure staff can believe in it and live that way. Apple exemplifies "thinking differently."

These values must connect how staff behave with what customers expect. Starbucks says, "our mission: to inspire and nurture the human spirit—one person, one cup and one neighbourhood at a time." Mark Bonchek (blogger) calls a shared purpose, "something that connects the way we make money and how we contribute to the world." For Nike, he states to bring ispiration and innovation to every athlete (if you have a body, you are an athlete)".

Values must be inherent in the DNA of a company. It is the values of the company that enables what it can do. They make it authentic.

The one thing that sets our brand apart

What sets a brand apart is often derived from the values that make the company unique.

The next layer we need to determine is the values that actually set us apart. This is less easy, and I often find that marketers stick to generic values that do not differentiate, or they fall into words like "innovative" – well knowing that very few companies can really claim that innovation is a core value.

What set our brand apart are the functional, emotional benefits offered by the category, focusing on those that we are able to offer uniquely. If nothing that we do is unique, we need to create differentiation in some other way, like the personality our brand has, or the icons or images associated with our brand.

Today, most winning brands are actually unique in fairly tangible ways – for example, Apple products are really uniquely designed: they look, feel and work differently. Amazon.com is really unique. Nowhere else do you have instant access to thousands of books at the touch of a key.

Typical questions to determine the uniqueness of our brand:
- What are the functional benefits?
- What are the emotional benefits?
- What are the generic benefits that all brands offer?
- What are the differentiating benefits that only our brand offers?
- What associations, words, images, symbols or icons are unique about our brand?

Once we have defined this uniqueness, it needs to be translated into the brand positioning. For that we have questions such as how we want to be positioned in the minds of our target markets, and what single-minded perception we want them to have about us. The simpler this is, the easier it is for staff and consumers to relate to and understand.

Before we move to the personality or kind of person the brand is, which is the next step in the generation of a brand strategy, let me explain in more detail the concept of positioning, because this is a key factor in successful brand performance.

Brand positioning

Brand positioning is one of the most important decisions any brand can make. Without that, it is very difficult to create marketing interventions that add brand value in a planned and consistent manner.

Positioning literally means the position a given brand name occupies in the minds of its consumers and other stakeholders. The nature of positioning is that no two brands can occupy the same space in the mind of a consumer, so by its very nature positioning means uniqueness. The term was made famous by Ries & Trout in the seventies.

The concept of brand positioning is similar to concepts such as unique selling proposition and differentiated marketing (choosing a unique angle no-one else is using and taking ownership of it). All these terms entail uniqueness. Positioning differs from brand image, which can be similar for many brands. All banks like to call themselves trustworthy or customer centric, yet not all bank brands are positioned.

Positioning thus refers to the single-minded perception the brand owner wants to create about the brand. Positioning needs to align with the brand idea, in that it needs to be short and simple and must encapsulate the brand idea. An example is Omo, the strongest washing powder for the cleanest wash.

A good positioning can easily translate into a brand promise: the reward to the consumer for using the brand. By using Omo, a consumer will have the cleanest laundry. This positioning may have many emotional benefits, such as a housewife feeling good about using the best for her family and a working mother needing to get the washing done with speed and ease.

Positioning is endorsed by elements such as:
- The reasons why a given positioning is credible and the brand owner is able to make a claim to its consumers.
- The pay-off line. This often encapsulates, in consumer terms, the brand promise. The best pay-off lines state the differentiator, as with:
  » DHL: We deliver, whatever it takes
  » Xerox: The quest for zero defect

- » HSBC: The world's local bank or
  » Mercedes-Benz: Engineered like no other car in the world.
- Often companies will use a brand personality – or tone – to reflect the kind of person a brand is, as with Virgin. It is a rebel and its tone is irreverence. With Toyota, it is leadership (the most reliable vehicles).
- All of the above is best summa-rised in what we call the brand essence. This is the fundamental differentiator for the brand. In the instance of Toyota, it is reliability. For Singapore Airlines, it is service quality. The brand essence must be short and truly unique. If you forget everything else about a brand, the essence is what remains important.

Positioning is not a pay-off line, something many people confuse. Yet, a strong positioning can result in a strong pay-off line. The overall positioning of Nike is that it is a brand that enhances and enables peak performance and has a can-do attitude. This translates into its pay-off line, Just do it. Every creative execution endorses this uniqueness.

Pay-off lines may change, but many people will say that it is easier to launch a new brand than to dramatically re-position an existing one. Positioning is a fairly fixed concept. Once it is decided, it should stay the same.

The degree to which re-positioning is feasible must be determined before any such change is made. Too big a positioning change may be impossible to effect. A brand owner always has to balance the possible increased revenue a change in positioning can bring about against the potential risk of losing existing customers if the change is too dramatic.

It is often easier to launch another brand into a new segment of the market, or into an area where a leading brand is being challenged. Fact is, it is better for a strong brand to cannibalise itself than for it to be attacked from the outside. If you "attack" yourself, you can manage the process. If you leave a gap for a competitor, you have no control over what they will do. In SA and Australia, Comair and Qantas did this well with their low-cost brands.

Many brands have added to their existing positioning, rather than changed. Swarovski crystals entered other categories but it still manufactures exceptional crystal. That remains the foundation of all it does. A brand like Nivea has done this well. It took its underlying positioning of caring for the skin into all it does today.

Some more questions to help you position your brand:
- How do I position my brand so that it maximises its opportunities in the marketplace and clearly differentiates itself?
- How can I redefine the competitive space?
- Is the positioning relevant to consumers?
- Can we establish the brand relative to the market, consumers and competitive constraints?
- Is my positioning credible and sustainable?
- Can I add to my positioning without

jeopardising its foundations? Do I know what these foundations are?

The personality of our brand

 Once you have determined the brand positioning, you need to outline the kind of person the brand is. In many markets, brand personality – or as it may also be called, brand tone – is a key differentiator for the brand. These two concepts are not identical, but they are similar. Generally, personality defines tone. The way a person speaks is a function of who the person is.

The more generic a category becomes, the more brands have to rely on personality differentiation.

Although Virgin Atlantic has been innovative in introducing firsts such as on-board massages, entertainment systems and limousine services, its major difference lies in the personality of the brand. This personality translates into everything the brand does, from its advertising, to its on-board announcements, to its on-board amenities, to its staff attitude. The fact that this attitude fits well with its positioning to always offer better consumer value enables it to have an irreverent personality.

These concepts must all align otherwise a brand strategy becomes more confusing than useful. Sadly, most such strategies I know are confusing.

Brand personality can also be called the brand attitude.

Typical questions to help us determine the brand personality are:

- Our personality depicts the kind of person we are as a brand. Are we aggressive, docile, friendly, challenging, energetic, passionate?
- It is difficult to act out of character, so to what extent does our value system determine the brand personality? A value system and the personality need to be aligned; they are not mutually exclusive. Brand personality determines tone: the way we speak.

The DNA or essence of our brand

Once we have defined the brand personality, we need to encapsulate that into a very powerful summation: a few words that describe the brand well and are the way the brand sets itself apart from others. This becomes the yardstick for all brand output. Ideally it should be one word, but that will take hard work and much debate. Yet, when we do this, it will simplify the overall vision of the company for all its stakeholders.

The single most important identifying and unique characteristic about our brand is the essence, also called the DNA. The nature of DNA is that it is unique. It determines and summarises all we are.

A BRAND ESSENCE IS LIKE A THUMBPRINT.

We have to consider what the totally unique DNA of our brand is and whether the DNA relates logically to the brand values, personality and positioning. If not, it is merely a set of words.

Always remember, simple strategies are difficult to do, complex strategies are easy to do. You just keep on adding words. Yet, it is very difficult to decide what is most important for a brand when you are faced with pages of words.

I had a professor who used to say some people talk until they say something. This is very true about most brand strategies except that – despite many words – most say nothing at all.

A simple acid test: if people read your strategy, will they understand your brand so well that they will be able to encapsulate who you are in five words?

How we want customers to respond to our brand

All this must translate into a particular take-out for the consumers. How must they respond to our brand if questioned? What will drive their purchase of our brand rather than any other brand?

Whereas most of the above relates to the stimuli we produce for consumers, this is about their response once they have been exposed to any part of our brand. Naturally, stimulus must lead to a desired response. This is another way to test if a brand strategy can be translated into something that is relevant to the consumers.

The response of consumers should be a function of how the brand is positioned, and the question to which we must find an answer should be something like: when stakeholders are exposed to our brand, what do we want them to say, feel, think and do?

Put together, the elements outlined above lead to a logical, integrated brand strategy.

Marketing

Strategy is important. Whilst this is not a treatise on strategy, a few pointers may be of use: Marketing strategy is important as it forces you to assess your brand status, make a decision about how you will grow it and give you rigorous guidelines to do so.

I still like the options Porter, later expanded by Moore, gave us:

1. Cost-leadership or mass = this is mostly for first-mover brands or ones that attained local and global saturation. This is the best position a brand can possibly be in. It means you will "sell" the generic attributes of the category (i.e. coverage, and quality if you are a cellphone network).
2. Differentiation = choosing an angle for your brand that will set it apart from others. This angle must be important for consumers.
3. Niche = Focusing on a segment of the market only.
4. Customer-focused = Putting the mechanisms in place to know and look after your customers better than any other brand.
5. Product design / technology focus = Using superior design (i.e. Samsung with flat screen televisions or Apple with iPads).

I find most companies do not have such a strategy, often not even implicitly. Trust me, it does help to guide marketing spend better. In the very least it does not hurt.

In a landmark article in *Harvard Business Review* in 1996 called What is Strategy? Michael Porter stated that operational effectiveness must not be confused with strategy. This is similar to the point made by Gary Hamel that most companies do their best to benchmark their performance against others instead of focusing on being different.

Porter said there was a debate that positioning is too stagnant a concept in an era where it has become so easy for one competitor to copy another. He stated that while operational effectiveness has become a fundamental aspect that businesses need to adhere to, it does not differentiate them.

A company needs to establish a difference it can sustain.

Porter then used the example of Southwest Airlines, whose positioning is to serve price- and convenience-sensitive travellers.

Its positioning is grounded in a whole list of doing things differently:
- The gate turnaround time is only 15 minutes, meaning that it could fly more often with fewer aircraft, providing more departures. This means the airline saves money by being more efficient and by having greater capacity utilisation.
- It does not offer assigned seating, food, interline baggage check-in or premium classes of service. This

simplifies logistics a lot and reduces the number of ways in which things can go wrong.
- The automated ticketing means passengers avoid travel agents, which saves Southwest commission.
- The use of a standardised fleet of 737's eases maintenance.

These factors mean Southwest is a unique business where all aspects of brand have an internal logic that offers a unique experience to customers at a unique cost advantage to the airline. It enables the brand to authentically offer the customer cheaper seats.

Hamel states that a good strategy is the most intellectually challenging thing a company can do. It is easy if your strategy is derived from that of another company but it is highly complex and challenging if you try to "create the different".

The bottom line is that different now translates into value and profit margin, more so than anything else. Apple is not the most valuable consumer goods brand on earth because it made a better mouse trap but because it creates unique products with a unique appeal. This is no different from Sony in the seventies and eighties.

SEVEN

BRAND NAME

AND IDENTITY

- A brand name is very important – it can make the marketing of a company inexpensive, fast, effective and efficient

- A great name becomes, in itself, a serious barrier to entry for competitors

- Yet most brand names are randomly chosen and badly thought through

- A brand identity must exemplify the name

- A good brand identity has inherent integrity in how it all fits together to differentiate the brand in the marketplace

What is in a name? Quite a lot more than we tend to think, I believe. The name and identity of a brand must be one of the most important decisions to be made about a brand. A good name and identity can buy the brand owner high impact at relatively low cost in a highly cluttered brand environment.

An average name will work if supported well with marketing expenditure. A good name can give the brand meaning straight away, saving it large investments in marketing communications to communicate and establish a brand name and identity that has no inherent meaning. It will work far better and at lower marketing cost.

The incremental benefit of a great name for a brand is very high, and it is one that deserves far more attention than we often pay to it. A name should not just be some random decision. I have truly experienced the impact of good names. Trust me, it works.

A brand name and its identity must be linked to form one whole concept. They are not mutually exclusive.

Brand names

In one of its client monographs, the global brand agency Interbrand states that a brand name is probably the most important of all elements of a successful product or service brand.

The reasons the agency cites are:
- A brand name becomes the holder of intellectual property rights. This is increasingly important today.
- The brand name captures the marketing investment in the name. The name thus becomes the receptacle for all the brand communications and other impressions. As with the name of a person, it stands for all that is good and bad about the brand.
- As with a person, a brand name gets associated with a certain personality. This personality is today one of

the most important sustainable aspects of a brand. Brands take on a unique set of perceptions. A brand can be serious, frivolous, irreverent, humorous, clever, trendy, confident, and a whole host of other personality traits.

- A brand name enables the identification of a particular product among competitors on a supermarket shelf, in the street or wherever the consumer wants to buy it. It also makes it possible to describe it in particular (Colgate) rather than as a product category (toothpaste). Without brand names, shopping would be very difficult indeed.
- A brand crosses linguistic and cultural barriers. In a global universe, brands cross all boundaries, so a brand has to remain meaningful within these, even if the way it is written may change (such as Coca-Cola). This has caused companies problems at times.
- Great brand names sometimes become part of our everyday language (think of Breakfast at Tiffany's).
- Brand names stick, even after they may have died. Brylcreem is a much less well-known brand today than it was 30 years ago, yet it is still known by certain people.
- Brand names represent the bond between consumers and an intangible entity. A brand name personifies an experience within a set of definitions. The brand therefore represents a set of associations.

Whereas a product will start as an unknown entity, giving it a name is similar to naming a child. It makes it unique and identifiable. Once a given name takes on a given meaning, the brand is positioned and it will become valuable. That is why a brand can also be called "a name with meaning".

Despite the importance of a brand name, I find most brand name decisions random and not well thought through at all, whether developed by brand owners or even proposed by brand agencies. When you have been in marketing for as long as I have, the "logic" of selecting a random brand name is difficult to understand, because I have seen the enormous value of well-defined names and identities. They create market impact, intrigue and a long-term brand perception, fast and easy, with a fraction of the marketing spend of standard brands. Yet, because most businesspeople rarely have to dream up new names, they do not understand the importance of this.

Even more important, a great name in itself becomes a serious barrier to entry for competitors, so its value is long term.

The name and identity of a brand must ideally encapsulate its positioning. The short-term insurance company Outsurance does this. The brand name signals it is out-surance instead of in-surance. The logo capitalises the three letters, O, U and T, emphasising what makes the brand unique. The pay-off line "You always get something out" endorses its positioning as the brand with which a consumer always gets something back – premiums are not just a bottomless pit.

Interbrand lists the following characteristics for a good name:

- It must be meaningfully differentiated.
- It must be appealing to the target market.
- It must have strong intellectual property rights to which the owner has legal title.
- It must be memorable.
- It must be easy to say and recognise.
- It must not have negative connotations, particularly for brands that cross language borders.

Neumeier states that the brand name Smuckers is effective because it sounds like the smacking of lips, suggesting a tasty jam. He states that powerful names combine the name with a strong visual icon.

Names can have many different origins. There are parentage names such as Cadbury's, Goldman Sachs and Disney; descriptive names such as Google, LinkedIn, Facebook and Vodafone; common names for created characters where the name implies a heritage (Jim Bean); and lateral names (Orange, Apple and Amazon.com).

There are very good examples of all of these working for brands.

My advice is to review the names in use in your category and apply the following principles:
- If you can create a new generic, do so. (A generic is a name associated with the whole category. For example, "Hoover" is used for any vacuum cleaner.) It will have imme-

diate and implicit meaning and it will take ownership of the category. Although a marketer may encounter some issues with a name being generic, the upside is better than the downside.
- If you can, use a name that will give the product inherent meaning, such as using a common name to signify heritage. Always remember that a non-descriptive name is more expensive to establish because you need to explain what the name means to consumers.
- Intriguing names work: it is unusual to call a computer Apple or a telecommunications company O2 or Orange. This alone evokes a debate and buys higher impact and share-of-mind.
- If heritage or parentage is the only way to differentiate a brand, use it. But remember that it will cost marketing money to establish the credentials of the chosen character (for example, Jim Bean). Once it is established, it is usually powerful and impossible to replicate.

Over the past few years, brand names have undergone noticeable changes. They have become shorter and simpler to express in more than one language.

Brand identities

A brand identity is the visual expression of the brand. It is also often called the shorthand for the brand.

Not all brands have an identity that is separate from its name (also called the logo). These days the way a brand name is written often becomes its identity. Google is a name, but the way it is written makes it an identity. The name is expressed in a particular – and proprietary – way, which is registered as the trademark of the brand.

Neumeier states that a logo was historically used by brand owners as a visual device to differentiate one brand from others in the same product or service class. He says a logo should be a repository of meaning, or an avatar that becomes a symbolic actor in a continuing brand story.

Adamson states that it is not always easy to express a brand driver verbally. Sometimes a visual expression can be very powerful.

Direct Line, a short-term insurer in the UK, uses the visual devices of a red telephone and a red computer mouse. The name, pay-off line and visual device of Nike work together to form one integrated brand identity. Anglo American takes ownership of the category of natural resources by using lines to portray mining contours. When we launched McCarthy Call-A-Car, we extensively used the icon of the telephone, and later the computer mouse, to take ownership of the distribution option. Today, icons are widely used by insurance companies to denote categories of insurance.

The Brazilian miner Vale uses a valley in its visual imagery, which is simply an expression of the name itself, signifying the roots of the company. Yet, this fact will not always be known. Companies often find it difficult to see a piece of communication from the vantage point of a customer. For customers, ensure that your communication will be understood. It is not their task to understand our brands – it is our task to communicate to them.

Because of the costs involved in marketing a brand, many companies today simply use the brand name instead of generating a separate logo. All else being equal, I agree with this.

One must accept that every single element of a brand needs to be communicated to its target audience. The more complex the pieces of communication that need to be conveyed, the more expensive it becomes to convey to the desired audience. That means simple is better. Establishing a name – and then also an identity – is expensive and complex, unless the two are entirely intertwined, which is rarely the case.

Clients have often asked me what the value of a good brand name and identity is. I have no doubt that a good name is worth a lot to a company. The name Outsurance – as taking ownership of a new way to insure your belongings – is powerful and forms a huge part of the impact of the brand. The name alone is a major part of its success, as it communicates its unique selling proposition as a brand. Yet, this is rare; most brand names do not do that.

Clients have also often asked me if the visual expression of a name really adds such tangible value to the brand that they should spend a lot of money on adapting it. What is the value of changing an identity? While I know the value of a good identity (Google) is very high, I also know that some changes in identity may have very little impact.

There has to be some realism about the impact of an identity. Decisions to change them need to be considered carefully, with clear objectives for what the new identity needs to achieve.

Sometimes companies expect too much of a new identity. Yet it can have a serious impact. Just consider how changing the "BP" identity to "beyond petroleum" and taking ownership of the colour green impacted the market share of the brand.

I fail to see the actual value from a business point of view when Pick n Pay adapted its identity. The cost of such changes, given the magnitude of it in terms of localities that need to be rebranded, is extreme. Unless such changes are accompanied by major changes in the company, one has to be realistic.

I understand why ABSA changed its name and identity after it merged 37 separate brands, which included four major bank brands – it had a serious business impact. But this is not always the case. I also know for a fact that while the marketing at the time worked well for ABSA, the organisational implications (people and systems) were far more complex and difficult to manage.

My advice to a CEO is to first address what the business imperative is for change, before a change is made for the sake of change. Then rather spend the money on more aggressive marketing.

Five things are important when considering brand identities:
- The name
- The typeface
- The brand logo
- The colours
- The tone, signified by the whole package

LET ME GIVE YOU EXAMPLES.

Virgin is a unique name. In fact, it works at least partly because it is so unusual. How can anyone decide to call a company "Virgin"? People will either like the unusualness of it or they may be offended by it (or even think it cannot be a serious brand with a name like that). But people will be intrigued by its unusualness and they are likely to remember it.

On top of that, the name is written in a highly unusual way, which endorses its uniqueness. It is also red – a bold, active colour that makes a statement. The tone of Virgin's advertising and other marketing communications, even on board its flights, is irreverent and bold.

These factors add up to make Virgin a highly significant brand that cannot be ignored by its audiences. Compare this with many other brand names for airlines that you can hardly remember.

When I ran my own agency, O2 Communications, the name itself spelled Oxygen (or a "breath of fresh air"). This name was also the initials of the two founders, both Oosthuizen: Anton and I. The name was intriguing and impactful. People noticed and remembered it. We used the Oxygen symbol as the logo. (Sadly we never registered it globally, as some years later a telecommunications company with the same name was launched in the UK. We would have made a fortune if we could sell the name and domain rights.)

The "For Dummies" series of books is a good example of an integrated name and identity. The name itself is a generic term often used when we refer to someone who knows very little about a given topic. Instead of being offensive, the name evokes a smile.

The For Dummies brand logo is unique and endorses this name: the blackboard signifies that we are going to learn something. The nerd character with his glasses endorses the tongue-in-cheek name and does so as something we make fun of. The character does not take itself too seriously. So even though some people may not like to be called dummies, they must smile when they look at the whole package. Yet, despite the playful tone, the content is great and useful to many.

The Nike swoosh is a right mark (as against a wrong mark). Together with the name, it has come to symbolise a brand with a particular positioning, which is personal performance. The pay-off line, Just do it, sums up this sentiment.

 The Nike name originates from the name of the Greek goddess of victory. The name alone takes ownership of a particular attitude. The three elements of the brand – the name, the logo and the pay-off line – reflect one integrated whole with a given marketplace positioning. This positioning is so strong that any one of these three elements could be isolated and still have the same impact as if they were all together.

This is rare in branding. But if a brand has that, it is an enormous asset. There is almost no way in which one can apply a value to the collective result. Within a highly cluttered brand environment, this is very important.

Another issue that is often raised by clients is whether a name that has become generic is still valuable or is simply no longer unique enough to be proprietary to a given brand. Examples of this are Colgate for toothpaste and Hoover for vacuum cleaners.

I have always had a simple counter-question to this: all else being equal, would you rather have a name that people know and understand, even though they may confuse other brands with it, or would you have a name that is unique yet more obscure, with lower levels of awareness and understanding? I think most owners of generic brands are happy for these brands to be generic, even though there are complications when it comes to brand communications, merchandising and other trade marketing output.

Finally, the kinds of questions brand owners must ask themselves:
- Does my brand name and identity maximise my competitive opportunity in the marketplace?
- Are there any changes I may want to make it clearer?
- Can the brand name and identity, ideally, express the positioning of the brand?
- Does the brand name and identity align with my business objectives?
- Can the name and identity, in its current form, enable me to achieve my objectives?

EIGHT

MARKETING THE BRAND:
THE MESSAGE

- First and foremost, all marketing communications need to give consumers a "reason why" to buy a brand

- Many brands have too many campaign messages

- Tell consumers why they must use your brand

- The message required to "keep" customers may not be the same as the message required to "get" customers

Marketing and sales go hand in hand. Many marketing people tend to underestimate the value of sales, but my experience is that if you have to choose, marketing needs sales more than the other way around.

Essentially, marketing must enable a company to retain and grow its business. Marketing communications play a vital role in achieving these objectives. As such, they are one of the most important components of effective brand management. They are often the component that costs the most money and has the most effect in growing a business fast. Great marketing communications have a significant multiplier effect on business.

Sadly, marketing is mostly run badly by companies with little logic, consistency or accountability. If this happens, it is extremely wasteful. Yet as wasteful as it is when done incorrectly, marketing is so powerful when used correctly.

I will deal with this broad topic of marketing the brand over four chapters.

To enable a brand to communicate well, certain key elements need to be in place. It must be agreed to whom the brand wants to communicate, and what it wants to communicate to them (the message).

A brand needs to communicate to its current and potential markets what makes it different from its competitors. It does this by using the tools of marketing communications such as advertising, packaging, publicity, online advertising, social media, events, promotions, competitions, sponsorships, product demonstrations and point-of-sale displays.

Three aspects are important when communicating to a market:
- A message that appeals to the current and potential markets of a brand – one that is relevant to their needs and easy for them to understand.
- How the message is creatively expressed to give it impact in the marketplace. Amid the vast number of marketing messages the average consumer is exposed to, only messages that are packaged in an impactful way will be noticed by the target-market consumers.
- The types of media that are used and how they are used in conjunction with other media.

Let us focus in this chapter on the message that has to be communicated. The next two chapters will deal with how the message is to be communicated and through which media, after which we will look at an integrated approach to selling the brand.

 ## The message

The message is what we tell consumers to persuade them to use our brand. It must address consumer needs and be simple to communicate and to understand. This may sound pretty easy, yet often it is very difficult. We may have to choose among different message options the one with the best potential to convince consumers.

There is a famous, yet deceptively simple, creative idea that was used to establish Lexus as the quietest car in its class. It shows a toddler sitting in his chair on the back seat of a Lexus with his mother driving. She asks him to tell her what sound a motorcycle makes, then what sound an aircraft makes. He perfectly mimics these, until she asks him what sound a car makes. Then he simply looks at her and keeps quiet. This is a simple and powerful creative idea. It clearly communicates that Lexus is the quietest car in its class.

Simple ideas are powerful, yet they rely on two important factors.

First, the message we need to communicate is distilled to its essence. Complex messages are not understood and often indicate that we made little effort to find the most appropriate message to convince our target market to consider our brand.

Second, the message must be expressed in a simple manner. As with the Lexus ad, great advertising is often simple. If a creative team from an agency needs to give you a lengthy explanation – or creative rationale as it is called – for the idea they present, it is not a good idea. A great idea needs no explanation; you just get it.

While I understand that there are instances where the production of an idea is complex so it will require some explanation when presented in its prototype format, ideas themselves must be simple to be effective. Always remember that consumers do not sit and watch our messages to try to ascertain what we are telling them. They have more important things to do.

When Dove soap was launched, and for many years thereafter, it used a simple idea of pouring velvety-soft cream into a bar of soap. That simply and clearly stated what makes the brand different. It is a simple yet powerful idea. It used the line, "Dove soap doesn't dry your skin because it's one-quarter cleansing cream".

Omo detergent, a Unilever brand highly successful in the rural areas of South Africa, used the simple line, "The strongest washing powder for the cleanest wash", suggesting that its highly active ingredient enables it to wash better than any other detergent. It made Omo the number one brand and created a very powerful barrier to entry for other detergents.

I have always believed in the principle that one message may not work for all target markets of a brand. We will often take the most powerful message as the key message for the brand, but as the brand grows and the large majority of the market gets saturated, we may need other messages to attract target customers who may have slightly different needs.

Yet all messages still need a central link to the positioning of the brand. If a message gets too distant from the positioning of a brand, it confuses customers. For me, the hierarchy of messages is like a family tree: they all come from the same root system.

What happens if a given message fails to attract consumers? If you tell people a joke and they do not get it, do not tell them the same joke over and over again. They either laugh the first time, or they do not laugh at all. The same applies to marketing messages: people either respond to a given message, or they do not. Do not keep on using the same message if it no longer finds any traction among the target market.

I have always used the same principle in advertising: if there is no evidence that a given message is liked and works, do not keep on spending money on it simply because you have the message. Marketing is expensive, so spend the money wisely. This means reviewing and deciding whether any given message works, not only based on gut feel or personal opinions but preferably on real market or consumer research evidence. Today, we often use the term "talk abil-ity" when a great campaign gets talked about spontaneously. This is difficult to orchestrate, but it is a very valuable outcome when it happens.

It is not always easy to find a message that works. A marketer needs to really understand his brand and what it offers to be able to find a unique angle. This may require many meetings, discussions and even focus groups discussing existing brands, their advertising and different features and benefits.

Consumers can give us pointers but they are generally not creative. They can only recite what they already know – which is what we told them about our brand and the category over the years. Very few consumers are able to give us more than that. At times it may be useful to have expert focus groups, or focus groups with people from different disciplines, or focus groups with people we label as trend-setters, to help us realise what message angles can work best.

Also remember that the very concept of differentiated marketing comes from choosing a given angle for the message, even though other brands may have the same benefits but may not have used that angle. I have seen many instances of this working. For example, many years ago FNB offered simple cheque accounts when no other bank was overtly doing so. Sometimes uniqueness can stem from simply talking about something that no other brand is talking about.

Today, FNB is spending money on significant messages to the market that offer the consumer something that FNB does better than the other banks. It is working. FNB is attracting large numbers of customers from the other banks. When you tell customers something they want to hear, they listen and respond.

While simplicity of message is one thing, a message also needs to be distinctive and unique. If not, we are selling the category, not our brand.

Let me give you an example. In South Africa, we have a plethora of short-term insurance companies that sell the consumer the best rates, so much so that it becomes very difficult to know which is the cheapest. The one that spends the most money and says it is the cheapest most often will inherit this space. That can be one or two companies, at most, which means that for the rest the message will, at best, be opportunistic, to gain a short-term advantage among the few people who happen to see it.

A problem among retailers is that often they focus only on price. If one is able to sustainably offer the best price, it is fine, but if not, it is a serious problem. Sooner or later another will have deeper pockets to be cheaper for longer.

Banks tend to fall into the same trap. Innovation in banks is rare, so most of their messages are generic: selling the same basic products and services at more or less the same price. This means the brand perception becomes the over-riding issue for banks, yet even there

the brands often fail to differentiate themselves.

Nokia spends a lot of money on marketing, talking about its smart phones. Unfortunately, unless it can do something that inspires the imagination of a technology-savvy world, like Apple does, it will remain a me-too smart phone brand. It does beg the question: why not provide a simpler and less costly version of a smart phone for less affluent consumers seeing that no other mobile brand can equal the global distribution network of Nokia? (They seem to have just entered this space now!)

Differentiation is the name of the game in marketing. In a complex and brand-saturated world, you need to offer something different to be noticed and to build a sustainable brand. The message is the key carrier of differentiation for the consumer, it is not something chosen at random.

Neumeier states, "If the communication in question looks as if it could have come from any other company or brand, then it is less than it could be." He calls the distinctiveness of a brand its voice (as in tone) – which makes the brand immediately recognisable.

Nike has one simple message it has used for many years: that Nike makes any performance possible for those who put their minds to it. Although it has used countless numbers of commercials over the years, they all essentially say the same thing.

NINE

MARKETING THE BRAND:
HOW TO EXPRESS THE MESSAGE

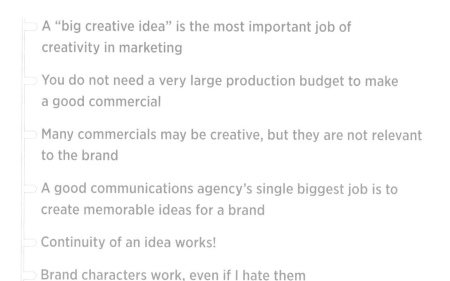

- A "big creative idea" is the most important job of creativity in marketing

- You do not need a very large production budget to make a good commercial

- Many commercials may be creative, but they are not relevant to the brand

- A good communications agency's single biggest job is to create memorable ideas for a brand

- Continuity of an idea works!

- Brand characters work, even if I hate them

In my experience, most communication inefficiencies come about because of:

- Too many campaigns;
- Too many messages;
- Messages that are not understood or well expressed;
- Too wide media usage;
- No clarity about the real source of sales;
- Low levels of differentiation in what is being said and how it is being said;
- No logic between campaigns; and
- No strong underlying DNA or positioning.

This is an area of huge opportunity for most brands.

Can the trade be used for greater effect relative to brand communications?

Once we know what we want to say, we need to express it in a way that will make the message stand out from the surrounding messages of other brands.

With many competing messages in the same and in other product and service categories, many of them with large budgets that can dominate awareness, it is imperative to ensure our message gets through to its audience. This is where creativity comes in.

The creative expression of the message remains one of the biggest challenges in marketing communications, and one that is the topic of much debate. Because creativity is by its very nature subjective, it is very difficult to get a definitive view on it.

I totally believe in the ability of a great creative expression to add enormous value to a brand. I have seen it many times. The ability of a great commercial to get noticed by its target market is many times that of an average commercial.

To give you an example, during the early nineties we launched a commercial for South African Airways showing tourist facilities in Europe preparing for South African visitors. The commercial was beautifully shot, with many exquisite locations being used.

Because of a very limited budget, this commercial was aired only a few times. After only three exposures, 9% of the South African public claimed that they had seen it. That is an extremely efficient result, way beyond the impact you can buy with many times that budget using an average commercial.
Since airtime costs the same for a good or a bad commercial, common sense suggests a good one is a far better investment for a brand.

Agencies will also often tell you that you need a very large production budget to be able to make a good commercial. This is simply not true. Great ideas can be produced fairly efficiently. The idea is what matters, supported by the production values and quality. But no amount of panel-beating will turn an average idea into a great one with good production values.

Another example is a highly impactful commercial VW produced for its Golf model. It showed a pilot earning his "wings" by a driving stunt in a VW Golf car. It was so popular that the commercial was aired less than once a week, yet in the Millward Brown Impact measurement it retained its high awareness for months on end.

Nando's, the iconic South African fast food restaurant chain, has also proved that spending less money than competitors can work if the creativity is exceptional.

Creativity works. To not have it puts a brand at a competitive disadvantage. Yet, how do you know it will work?

Many commercials may be creative, but they are not relevant to the brand. This can work once a brand is well established, but early on in the life of a brand, it is dangerous, because people will remember the content but forget the name of the brand. This is often the case when we use celebrities in commercials. Unless there is a clear link between the celebrity and the brand, often the name of the celebrity will be remembered while the name of the brand will be forgotten.

Sometimes a commercial uses visuals that do not connect back to the words. In such instances, people will remember the visuals far better than the words. Some research suggests that up to 85% of a television commercial is noticed because of what is seen: the people, where they are, what they wear, what they do.

Many commercials use fast cuts, showing many locations and ideas in a 30-second spot. I have found that most people find this very confusing, except for very young people who are used to a staccato style of doing things.

Many brands change their creative content all the time. Working on Toyota, we once produced a commercial for Corolla that was so different from any other commercial we had made for the brand that when we conducted research among the desired target market, people did not even see the commercial was for Corolla. This was a waste of money.

Consumers seem to expect a certain tone from a commercial. If it is too close to the tone of another brand, or if we keep on changing the tone from one commercial to the next, consumers will not associate it with our brand. This sounds crazy, but I have seen this happen many times. This is very true for brands that are not yet well established, that compete against a very dominant competitor, or that have no consistency in their tone. New brands have to be very careful of this problem.

Theme consistency works. If you use the same characters and themes all the time, it becomes associated with the brand, which means every new commercial that is aired is immediately associated with the brand. This is very useful.

Vodacom used the same characters for many years in South Africa, highly successfully. Dulux uses a dog as a branding device very successfully. The Michelin Man has been used for over 100 years for the same reason. M&M's uses cartoon characters. MTN used the expression "Ayoba" in many campaigns. Yet, as with everything in life, there is a caveat. If such devices are used too much, they will lose their effect. Consumers will simply see all commercials for the brand as saying the same thing.

Sanlam experienced this many years ago when it used babies in its commercials. These were very successful (children and animals always work in commercials), yet people saw the commercials in the name of Sanlam but did not hear the message. The sheer dominance of the visual impact over verbal impact meant that all the commercials sold the Sanlam brand, while the individual messages about products and services got lost.

For Sasol Oil, we used another approach. We retained the message and tone, selling the performance gained by using Sasol, in a particular South African hyperbole idiom. None of the commercials was exactly the same (in that they did not use the same characters, for example), yet they all had very high target-market impact and were liked a lot.

We used a toy car that accelerates very fast when filled up with Sasol. This fascinates the boy playing with the car and he shakes it to find out what has happened. This commercial won a gold medal at the Cannes advertising festival. Another commercial showed grandparents around a baby in a pram whose first word is "Sasol", after which the pram accelerates very fast, startling them.

These commercials were very successful and made Sasol the most noticed South African fuel brand for many years. I learnt a lot by working on Sasol. We were even able to decrease the advertising expenditure over the years because the impact of our commercials was so great.

The global research company Taylor Nelson many years ago devised an approach it believes works: a great creative idea holds the message of an advertisement and the brand together in such a way that it can only be for a given brand.

The big idea

Unilever uses the term "big idea", which refers to the creative way in which the brand message is conveyed. Very few advertisements or other forms of brand communications have big ideas, hence the overall level of impact from brand communications is low. Some research suggests that less than 5% of marketing communications is actually noticed by its target market.

In my experience, this is true. Very few communications campaigns actually achieve an impact factor that is greater than the investment made in the campaign. A great creative expression achieves far more impact in the marketplace than a similar yet less impactful message with the same marketing investment. The creative way in which a message is expressed therefore significantly determines the value for a given media investment.

SO WHAT IS A BIG IDEA?

A simple example of a big idea was BMW's launch of power steering in all its cars in South Africa many years ago. It used a small white mouse to run around the steering wheel of the car and thereby turn it – a simple demonstration of how easy it is to drive the new BMW with power steering. This commercial won a gold award at the Cannes advertising festival as well as many other global awards.

AT&T ran a series of commercials in the US to demonstrate how easy it was to use an iPhone to find information, to find opinions about products, to contact friends for their advice before buying, to search online for the best price for the product, and then to buy and pay online. This was a series of simple demonstrations, done in a highly entertaining way.

The Old Spice campaign outlined on pages 120 and 121 in this book is a big campaign idea. It achieves high impact with a relatively low investment in media. The idea is memorable and it can be extended into many different expressions, while it retains the central creative idea. Its ability to extend is almost limitless.

The Nokia visual device of touching hands is a really big creative idea because the brand takes ownership of human interaction. It signifies all the symbolism that is associated with human interface. The idea is memorable and instantaneously recognised as the visual device of Nokia. The value of such a symbol for a brand is high. I am not sure why Nokia does not use this symbol more. It is a great property to own.

The bottle shape of Coca-Cola is unique. It resembles a cocoa bean. Using it enables Coca-Cola to take category ownership of a cocoa bean. No other brand in the cola category can do that because the image is owned by Coca-Cola.

Over many years, *The Economist* has used a particular brand attitude and creative expression of that. It uses for its masthead white copy reversed out of red to express its attitude of one-upmanship. Those who read *The Economist* are brighter, more competitive and more informed. You either read *The Economist* or you are in the wilderness of ignorance. But the magazine does it in a clever way; it is not rude or confrontational. In fact, much of it is tongue-in-cheek and funny.

Absolut Vodka uses a unique bottle shape to differentiate what is largely a parity drink. (There is little difference between the tastes of different brands of vodka, hence we can call them "parity" offerings.) The visual of a bottle has been used as a creative carrier for generations.

When BP changed its name from British Petroleum to "beyond petroleum", it signified the change with a new logo of a stylised sunflower. That was a big idea, even if it was tested by the oil spill in the Gulf of Mexico some years later. Taking ownership of the colour green led to high impact and visibility for the brand, as well as an increase in market share in several markets.

MTN uses the colour yellow to its advantage in Africa and the Middle East. The impact of yellow in environments that are often poor and colourless is significant. Yellow is bold, has a high impact and suggests a certain attitude. It is a significant colour to own – not since brands such as Kodak and Hertz has any brand used yellow as extensively in its markets.

Great ideas can also suggest tone: the movie director Tim Burton, who was responsible for movies including *Edward Scissorhands* and *Alice in Wonderland*, has a unique creative style. His characters are immediately identifiable.

Rolex uses iconic global personalities who put exceptional performance first and who place very high demands on themselves.

Great ideas make a brand immediately identifiable. When we see a Virgin Atlantic advertisement, we immediately know it is one.

Identifiable characters

Over the years, some brands have used identifiable characters in their advertising to make them memorable. One of the most famous is the Michelin Man. KFC uses the face of its founder, Harland Sanders, known as the Colonel. I have found this very useful because the target market immediately identifies a piece of communication as connected to a given brand.

Vodacom established its brand as a South African icon through the use of the same two characters in all its advertising over many years. Another famous local example is the way in which Castrol used two characters in its advertising for many years.

With these, even if one execution in the series was not as good as another, it still achieved high impact. That certainly suggests consumers become more receptive to the brands they enjoy, endorsing the principles of selective exposure and selective retention.

The biggest single job a good communications agency does for a brand is to create memorable ideas for it. The value of defining a brand and making it instantaneously memorable is immeasurable. Unless an agency can do that, I am not sure what an agency can do, because that is the imperative for the industry: to create talked-about ideas.

DRUMS criteria

I have developed a simple way to judge advertising that I call the DRUMS criteria for evaluating creative work:

- Different: The advertisement is different from others in the same product or service class. This enables it to stand out. Is it different enough to be noticed, yet still relevant to the brand? (Although a naked person in any advertisement will be noticed, it may not be relevant to what is being sold.)
- Relevant: The advertisement is relevant to the needs of target-market customers. Does it address a consumer need? Surely this is the basis of all communication, yet as brands get older, even bizarre messages may work, like the famous Cadbury slab Gorilla commercial. This is more challenging while the brand is still being established.
- Understandable: The advertisement is understandable and therefore simple in what it communicates. This is very often violated. Great ideas are often deceptively sim-

ple, but when you have to explain too much, it is likely to be lost on the target audience. Even though consumers may be very clever, they simply do not bother that much to find out what we try to tell them in our advertising.
- Memorable: Is it memorable – is it a big idea that will linger? As the costs of marketing increase, we want the target market to remember the advertising until the next time they see it. Most advertising is forgotten fast. The more memorable the advert is, the better.
- Smile: Does it make consumers smile, laugh, cry or act? What behaviour do we expect from consumers after they have seen the commercial?

This is where creative themes help a lot. The principle of "ad stock" by Rosser Reeves (academic and advisor to the Ted Bates agency) tells us that a brand builds up a certain level of awareness for its advertising, and every subsequent commercial adds to that. The lowest level it drops to is what he calls the ad stock.

Great advertising builds the ad stock through being memorable. Bad advertising undermines the ad stock. The challenge is to build ad stock slowly and incrementally, because a too-serious decline will cost a lot to rebuild. On the other hand, when we spend far too much money, we face diminishing returns.

In my estimation, when reviewing the research results from companies like Millward Brown, over 85% of advertising does not get noticed by enough consumers to create any residual ad stock. This means the vast majority of advertising may be wasted.

I have seen how memorability enables brands that are call-centre driven to get calls outside the periods when commercials are being flighted – far more so when the advertising is thematically linked or has high impact levels. For brands such as Sasol Oil and McCarthy Call-A-Car, we aired commercials based on their level of retention. The greater the level of retention, the less often we need to flight the commercial.

The landmark research by the US Advertising Research Foundation in the nineties supported the long-term brand-building role of marketing, and the principle that building a brand becomes less and less dependent on one given exposure. Successive marketing interventions (advertising, social media, sponsorships, packaging) in a defined direction build the brand over time.

A last note on creativity: as a marketer it is important to expose yourself to new thinking. If the agency presents you with a creative concept that you feel comfortable with because it is safe, it is not good enough. The chances are that if you feel it is safe, the audience will not even notice the commercial because it is too safe.

TEN

MARKETING THE BRAND:

MEDIA CHOICE

- Using media is also about retaining or growing your customers: Decide where the focus is, and select accordingly

- If a budget is limited, rather reach fewer people more often

- Social media is not just an add-on. It needs to be integrated with other media. Fundamentally, you as the brand owner need to address a lot of strategic issues when using social media

- In all media "content" rules!

Most of the budget of most marketers is spent on media. The media decision is thus of extreme importance for a marketer. The choice is wider than ever, including print, radio, television, the various types of internet media and cellphones. With so many options, deciding how to reach the desired target audience is not easy.

Media are the conduits within which we package our creative messages, and we need to reach a required target market often enough to convey a given message. Even one person telling another is a medium, and its impact can be much greater than when the same message is conveyed through a television or print advertisement.

Historically, the mass media was the most potent way of reaching a large number of people. Many people would remember the high impact of commercials like the "1984" Apple commercial aired at the Superbowl in the US. This single airing put Apple on the global map.

Global sports events such as the Olym-
pic Games and the Soccer World Cup still have this kind of power. But times are changing and although the mass media still have a role, types of media like viral marketing and social media are becoming more and more important.

 It is mooted that social media will soon be 50% of the media spend in developed countries. What still holds social media back in emerging countries is a lack of general access to these media, but that is changing fast. Among the higher-income educated consumers in these markets, access already equals that in the developed world.

In many ways, my experience has been that emerging countries are leapfrogging developed countries in the importance of these media. This is at least partly because these countries do not need to unlearn behaviour because few other channels of communication have been available to date; these consumers are young and more open to new ways of doing; and these consumers want to be a part of the global universe. The emerging country populations are also generally more sociable people than those often found in the developed economies. Family and friends are simply more important.

Media selection is mostly based on critical mass. We select the types of media that will reach most people fast and cost effectively. Yet, this is not the only important issue.

For me, three things determine media selection:
- The most economical way to reach the defined target market;
- The involvement of the target market with the media; and
- The way in which the creative expression is able to leverage the media best in how the message is expressed.

There are two main considerations when making media decisions:
1. **Reach** – we need to decide how many people in the defined target audience we want to reach. Reach is often what makes a given medium expensive. The types of media that reach many people in a defined market are expensive. Cheaper media generally reach fewer people, except for specialist media that reach very selective audiences (for example general practitioners in a specialist publication).
2. **Frequency** – we need to decide how many times we want to reach this audience in a defined period. If we reach them too sparsely, we will lose all impact; if we reach them too often, we will reach diminishing returns fast. Both of these waste money.

It is important, in my view, to reach a consumer at least once a month through most media. That means more frequent exposure since a few exposures will translate into one actual reach, because of the difference between opportunities to see and actually seeing the commercial.

Some studies suggest you have to have three to eight opportunities to see before you will actually see the commercial once. This is where a great creative idea will help: the better the idea, the faster that one opportunity to see will translate into at least one actual viewing. A great idea will also be remembered for longer, which makes it even more economical.

The balance between reach and frequency is important: if your marketing budget does not allow a desired audience reach to be achieved with a reasonable frequency, drop your reach requirements and rather reach fewer people more often.

To reach very many people once may not work, because many people will see without really noticing. One exposure is not enough. Most messages need more than one exposure to be noticed by target-market consumers. The retail sector is different, and you may simply want a number of people to see a special offer once, but retail is a category with many such unique issues.

Two important lessons I learnt many times in marketing are: If you spend money on marketing, it works. If you tell consumers something they want to know, it works.

When I launched the Service Excellence in Banking campaign for Volkskasbank, the bank had a small market share and needed to grow. It needed to attract more customers of the right profile, and the mass media is great for achieving growth on a large scale.

We invested heavily. Overnight, the bank became one of the top 10 highest advertising spenders in South Africa. We spent R1.5 million a month on advertising at the time, more than brands such as Rothmans. It worked. We increased our rate of attracting new clients by 95% year-on-year. We also attracted the right profile of customers.

We monitored this campaign day by day, using the typical (at the time) American day-after-recall study. We monitored how many people saw every new commercial and we monitored their take-out, propensity to act and actual actions. I learnt the vital importance of knowing what is going on and taking responsibility for your actions in marketing.

With many other advertising campaigns, assisted heavily by my good friend Erik du Plessis, founder of Impact Information, today Millward Brown South Africa, I learnt that you need to spend enough money to break through the competitive clutter. Unless you do that, you do not establish a new campaign in the minds of your target audience.

Reach is vital. It is a predecessor to everything else in marketing communications. You can remind people only once they have seen something at least once. I learnt that the good way (by launching campaigns well) and the bad way (by spending too little money and having to do it again). Whatever you do, make sure your launch works.

Impact started a new methodology at the time that tracked every new commercial after launch. Impact determined how many consumers saw a new commercial one week after launch. It then asked how much people liked these commercials. Generally, the more they liked a commercial, the greater the number of people who could recall it. This means creativity works. The more creative a commercial, the greater its ability to break through the competitive clutter and the greater its awareness level for the same amount of money spent.

I also learnt how bad creativity can cost you money. We made a commercial in which the then chairman of United Building Society told customers, in a two-minute commercial, why United had decided to become a listed company. It was one of the lowest-noted commercials ever in South Africa. Despite spending a fortune airing it, hardly anyone liked or remembered it when we researched it. You cannot bore people into listening to you. The fact that we think something is important does not mean others do.

During my advertising days I learnt that you need to spend money to obtain results, up to a point. Great advertising will work far better, but even average advertising will work if you spend enough money. This is the philosophy that has built many fast-moving consumer goods brands.

When you wanted to make an impact, television used to be the best medium to reach many people fast. It was good for launches. For any launch, reaching critical mass fast to create a barrier to entry for competitors is important.

Today we use other types of media, but the principle remains that a new brand or campaign needs to spend money in high-reach media to make an impact. This can be supported by lower-reach media, but never at the expense of reaching many fast. Other types of media are good with other things, but electronic media still dominates awareness.

Over the years, I learnt that simply switching the ratio of spend between television and print advertising significantly impacted brand awareness levels. The higher the spend on television, the greater the impact on awareness – up to a point. Yet, this does not mean print advertising is less important. Many great brands are built using mainly print advertising. Consistent print seems very powerful.

Historically, we know that certain types of media are better at doing certain things. At the risk of over-simplification, here are some broad pointers:

- Generally, it is accepted that television is good at conveying emotion and feeling. It also buys high impact fast.
- Print advertising seems more powerful with detail and when a lot of information needs to be conveyed. It is also good for showcasing a product or service.
- Radio advertising is often seen as good at constantly reminding an audience of a message or brand. In South Africa, radio advertising has become expensive because there are so many different stations that may be required to reach enough of a given audience.
- Outdoor media is useful for reminding people of brands or even for establishing brands in defined locations.
- Direct communications and social media are great for changing people's perceptions and opinions. The more directly targeted a message, the better the chance it will work. Decades of political house meetings have proved that. Today, the social media play this role on a wider scale.
- Experiential marketing and social media are good at inducing usage in new markets. People like to touch and feel a brand, more so if it is something like a car.
- Social media endorse usage and can be very good for sales leads and in spreading the word.
- Brand demonstrations and coupons are used for encouraging consumers to try a new brand. They work to reduce the risk of the trial.
- Loyalty and reward programmes are important in creating brand loyalty. But these programmes must amplify good service rather than try to patch a leaking tank.
- Sponsorships create brand affinity. Together with the mass media, sponsorships create awareness among people. This is even more powerful when we try to establish new brands or new ideas.

Generally, it is easier to achieve reach fast among young people. They notice and decode advertising much faster, all else being equal. It is also easier to establish perceptions where none exist than to change perceptions once they exist.

Advertising can be controlled fully. Because you "buy" advertising, you have more control over how much of it you get – which is not the case with social media or publicity. As a result, advertisements are powerful builders of perceptions fast.

WHY DO MOST COMPANIES USE SOCIAL MEDIA INCORRECTLY?

Consumers do not engage with social media to be sold brands. They use it to keep contact with, interface with, engage with and resonate with the things, people and issues they like, love and want to deal with.

Most brands use social media almost as shopfronts or websites: they repeat the same content, just in another format, over and over again. This misses the entire underlying philosophy of social media as a tool for communities of interest, to engage on their own terms, without anyone abusing it. You do not expect to be sold a life policy when you have dinner at a friend's house. Similarly, social media must integrate a brand in ways that are relevant to the brand and relevant to the issues surrounding the brand. It must not be deliberately "planted".

Most Facebook pages simply replicate website pages, most tweets from brands

HELLO?

are hard sell, most YouTube posts from brands are posted by their agencies or marketing departments. Even on sites such as Hello Peter, one wonders how many comments are placed by staff.

A company needs to think strategically about how it places its customers at the centre of its being and organisation, and then see how social media is applied. It needs to be honest and authentic and should not disguise mistakes. It must excite customers through other customers, in unique, entertaining, inspiring and informative ways. CONTENT rules. If the content of the brand is original, it will engage people and it will add value to their lives.

This means a lot of strategic changes in structure and the way in which brands interface with their customers.

A marketer also cannot say he will not engage. You are engaged in social media, like it or not. It is up to the company to ensure it can use social media positively to become part of the "actuality of daily life" for a brand. This changes every single aspect of the brand – it makes it all immediate and it makes news old very fast.

A marketer cannot really "manage" social media in the same way as he would do with most forms of marketing. He needs to plant the right stimuli with the right people.

Pointers for marketers on social media:
- Unlike any other marketing activity, it will change the way the whole company works.
- It needs immediate and

ongoing management by people empowered to engage with customers about anything at any time.

- It needs strong content creation and management, about issues that add meaning, truth, information and actuality to the lives of people and those close to them.
- It must engage with communities about the issues of importance for them. The brand is, at best, a conduit for that. So if a brand excites the consumer anyway, social media will work for you, regardless of whether you manage it well or not.
- You must really know what makes your customers tick: who they are, what they like, what they do, who they talk to, what interests them, what they read and what they do at night. You need deep insight into them and their behaviour.
- You need to be truthful or you will be found out.
- You need to be hands-on; you cannot fully outsource social media to an agency.
- You need to be on the ball – globally, all the time, with issues you can leverage.
- You need to make sure that, when brands are spoken about, yours is the topic. But that will only happen because you do novel and engaging things, not because you try to optimise searches, as in the past.
- You need to know the media as they are added to, because the terrain is very dynamic and changes from day to day. The terrain is also highly fragmented, so you need to be where it matters, all the time.
- You need to use data and measurement as far as possible: know how your customers and potential

customers engage, where, how, why and why not.
- Data and content are the new kings and queens.

SPONSORSHIPS

It is often claimed that sponsorships add the "heart" aspect to brands – in other words, by supporting a particular event, a brand "cares" for the people that care for the event or activity. In that sense, one can say that even though a large sponsorship will increase awareness for a brand (for example, Hyundai sponsored the World Cup, which increased global awareness for the brand), it is often done to make consumers who love the sport or event more loyal to the brand.

A big problem with sponsorships is that many events have too many sponsors. Then you either have to be far bigger or spend far more money to be noticed. Just being another sponsor is not good enough, unless you use the sponsorship for corporate entertainment or you combine it with other events to attract customers.

The more that sponsorships are integrated with activities at retail and experiential level, the better. In South Africa, Standard Bank has done very well by linking its sponsorship of cricket to its advertising and other marketing activities.

I believe in a few key principles when it comes to sponsorships:
- Be clear on why you are doing it – whether it is to create awareness, to entertain customers, to liaise

with customers, to attract more of a certain type of customer, etc.

- Do less, not more. Companies that focus on bigger activities and events achieve more success than companies that sponsor many smaller things.
- Dominate the activity as much as you can.
- Try to get naming rights. Media-coverage rights are also very important.
- If need be, design your own sponsorships.
- Integrate with other marketing activities, right down to sales activation and experiential marketing.
- Do not change once you choose. Stick to your sponsorships because it takes time to build a sustainable presence.

The objectives of a campaign are critical when selecting media. Marketers often remain focused on mass media and only dabble in other media. Media decisions must be derived from business decisions: what do I want to achieve and what media are best for that?

When a market is saturated, surely the need for mass communications such as television and print diminishes and the use of direct communications, experiential marketing and social media needs to increase. That said, when we launch a new brand or product with a wide audience, we may still need the mass media in some segments and communities to reach critical mass.

I buy the principle that some campaigns need mass media support even when they are targeted at small groups. Cabriolets are often used by car companies to sell the glamour of the brand, even though very few people will buy them. Mobile telephone companies use innovation in the same way to sell the superiority of their brands. This may mean a media decision looks illogical on the surface, yet it has other objectives.

To plan media well, I always think it is best to start with the objectives for the year, and leave a small amount of money for tactical spend. If that is not done, we often end up with no strategic direction in how we spend the money – with a loss of our key objectives.

The chosen media need to work together to project one whole brand perception to the target audience. When an audience is not literate, we need the visual impact in store to be identical to what they have seen outside, because recognition rather than words will then make them buy when they enter a supermarket.

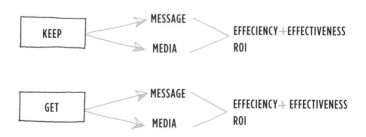

ELEVEN

MARKETING THE BRAND:

INTEGRATED APPROACH

- Integrated marketing really works – and it requires active management by brand owners

- Integrated marketing is far more than making a print ad from the end frame of a television commercial

- Agency briefs are vital. They must be simple and answer the question "why?"

- The trade is critically important in marketing, yet as marketers we often do not recognise it

- Although marketing may have pulled consumers towards your brand, it is the trade experience that will make them buy and buy again

- Do I give consumers substantive reasons to believe my claims?

- All media tools have strengths and weaknesses; use them to amplify one another

- Brand activation and similar tools are vital to grab consumers by "the scruff of the neck and make them buy": They make consumers experience the brand "end-to-end"

The concept of integrated marketing communications is over 40 years old. Yet, in my experience, it is still rarely practised.

If it is practised, it is through using the central advertising idea as the core of the entire campaign. This is not necessarily wrong, but it may not be the best way to do it in a given instance, as the choice of media must be driven by your objectives.

It is important that the types of media we select all join forces to communicate 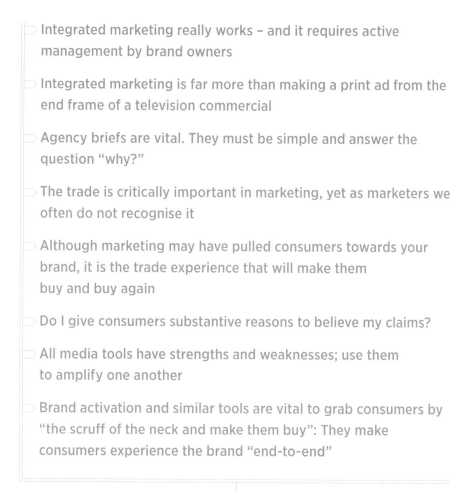 the positioning to the consumer. The better these tools are integrated, the more they portray one overall message from the brand. The less they are integrated, the more likely that the brand will confuse the consumer.

Aligning brand communications with other aspects of marketing communications like packaging, promotions and sponsorships has a significant impact. The greater the integration, the greater the impact and the greater the efficiency of media selection. Let me give you three examples that I was involved in where we worked very hard at integrating the campaigns.

When we launched e.tv, we wrote a central marketing, trade and brand strategy and aligned all aspects of our output. We did the central thinking and planning, and used a wide network of specialists to execute it.

We designed the brand identity, we designed and executed the on-air promotions, we sat together and reviewed every programme to enable the best marketing angle, we wrote every programme insert with the assistance of suppliers, we made, on average, 120 radio and 60 print commercials a month. We produced the trade elements. The only two things we could not take credit for were the corporate publicity and launch event.

When we launched AngloGold (that was before Ashanti came into the fold), we did the same thing. We decided what we wanted to do and sourced all the facets of the campaign. My two colleagues at the time, Thys Botha (who managed the whole project) and Pami Preller (the creative elements) managed every single supplier, every day, on every element.

There were over 300 separate elements that had to be done, from the new brand name and identity (conceived by Bobby Godsell, the CEO at the time) to the advertising in key global business media, to the internal launches on four continents, to all stationery, invitations and the launch at the New York Stock Exchange, where a live lion was taken

 onto the trading floor.

Every single element looked exactly the same, yet they all had a high impact in their own right. Integrated marketing is about far more than making a print ad from the end frame of a television commercial, as most agencies do. I was taught that integrated marketing should have visual similarities to enable direct image transfer, but every element must still suit the medium in which it is executed. This campaign was hugely impactful and won a number of global below-the-line awards at the time.

The third example was when Comparex, a large information technology company, merged with Business Connexion to form the new Business Connexion. I handled the central strategy for the launch. We worked with a large team of suppliers, which was managed with a firm hand. Every single element was presented, discussed and approved at the weekly status meetings. The CEO and the executive were involved in the strategy.

The campaign consisted of a brand valuation, a new corporate identity, a new advertising campaign, a direct campaign to all customers, a personal visit and telephone call to key customers, and countrywide client and staff events that were all linked through a satellite broadcast. Even competitors of Business Connexion complimented the company on the merger launch.

These kinds of activities taught me some important lessons about integrated marketing. It requires a strong and clear strategy to hold everything together. It requires strong management from the client or an independent person not linked to any one supplier of output. It requires regular meetings of all participants – without exception. It requires rigid standards of execution and integrated ideas. It requires that the process is not run by the advertising agency, which often fails to be neutral or media agnostic.

Briefing the agency

Agency briefs are very important, yet they are often overlooked or even dismissed.

The client needs to tell the agency what message it wants to convey. Although the actual content of an agency brief will depend on company and agency requirements, a brief needs to have exactly the right amount of information to be of use to an agency. If it has too much information it will confuse the creative team in the agency. If it has too little, they will not be able to do a proper job.

Many marketers are far too relaxed about briefs. A good brief needs to be done well, it needs to be on paper, and it needs at least the following:

- Background on the brief, the brand and the product or service the brief is about;
- How the brand, product or service differs from those of competitors;
- The objectives of the campaign, both in marketing (what sales objectives need to be achieved) and in communications (how many people need to be reached and what level of awareness for the campaign needs to be created);
- The target market for the campaign in as much detail as possible, demographically, psycho-graphically and in lifestyle;
- The message the brand needs to convey that will make target-market consumers buy;
- The tone of the message (how it needs to be expressed), which stays true to the brand overall but can vary slightly to suit the given campaign and its intended target market (for example, a commercial directed at young people will differ from one directed at older people);
- What is required (advertising, online, social media, posters, brochures, direct mailers);
- The timing requirements; and
- The budget parameters (what money is available in total).

A good brief is really important – it also provides a template to judge the creative outcome. It ensures everyone is on the same page. Bad briefs are often responsible for the breakdown of client–agency relationships. Many clients are slack about this. Many marketers have fallen into the trap of simply passing on their responsibilities to the agency, with very little thinking from their side.

A good brief takes time and requires in-depth insight and thinking. All agency brief documents should be approved by the marketing director as it is ultimately his responsibility. In most instances, it constitutes the bulk of the marketing budget.

Sales and trade activation

Let me say right away that I am not a trade or sales expert. But I do know these elements are the most vital aspects of any company. Many marketing people tend to be dismissive of sales. You do that at your peril. Without them, we can do the most amazing things but they will not work.

To be frank, if a company cannot spend any money on marketing, a good sales team can save the day and keep the company in business. For this reason, marketing needs sales more than sales need marketing, although some may dispute this.

You may recall that a brand such as Woolworths was already large before it started advertising. Yet, without good-quality products it probably would never have made it that far. But when the product is good, great marketing adds exponential value that creates valuable brands. So marketing is an important strategic investment for a company.

The above may be a somewhat simplistic argument, but the point is that marketing and sales also need a well co-ordinated and integrated approach.

The trade relationship of the brand, relative to its competitive status and marketing status, is vital as this is often a gap. A stronger trade presence, with greater impact, can overcome a smaller marketing budget. But then we need to know where to focus.

By simply changing its identity and without changing its numeric distribution much, BP increased its market share years ago.

By simply focusing on the best campaign and on high-impact media, we increased brand awareness for a fuel and an automotive brand.

Most consumers will experience a brand only at trade level, when they enter a retail outlet. This is where the actual buying takes place. This also applies to the internet. Although marketing may have pulled them towards the brand, it is the trade experience that will make them buy and buy again.

In Diagram 7, I list the types of questions you need to ask about the brand in the trade.

DIAGRAM 7
HOW AVAILABLE THE BRAND IS AND HOW IT IS
PRESENTED TO THE CUSTOMER IN THE TRADE:
TYPICAL QUESTIONS

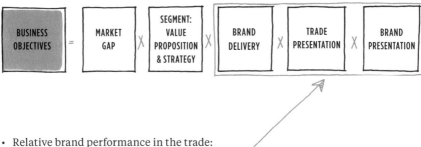

- Relative brand performance in the trade:
    How available is your brand where consumers want to buy it?
    How available is your brand relative to where most people live/shop?
- Relative to trade impact:
    How visible is your brand relative to its competitors (eg. MTN's yellow stands out).
- To what extent are we assisting purchasing?
    Do we have the right signage to indicate where consumers can buy?
    Do we have the right point of sale material? Do we have the right displays in store?
- Do we have trained and informed staff?
- Does the trade make it easy for consumers to buy?
    Does the brand stand out on the shelf? Does it stand out even when people cannot read?
    Do we make it easy for consumers to try the brand?

A marketer needs to ask the following kinds of questions when dealing with the trade:

- How do people know where they can buy our products and services?
- How well are these signposted?
- When people enter these stores, will they know where to go to enquire about what they want? How often do you walk into a store without having any idea where to go for what you want?
- Are the staff trained to serve customers properly? Do they know how to greet them and listen to them?
- Are the staff sufficiently empowered to have some degree of latitude about offering customers deals and options, or must they ask a more senior person every time?
- Are the staff informed about current promotions and specials?
- Does the store have stock of what it advertises? Are the staff trained in these products?
- Are the goods on display in a way that customers can view them and read about them?
- Does the staff know what to do if a given item is not in stock? Can they up-sell or manage a problem, such as being out of stock, in a way that doesn't make it the customer's problem?
- Do the staff close the deal in a way that will incline the customer to return to the store?
- Do staff members use their initiative? How often have you eaten at an airport restaurant and then waited so long to get the bill that you have almost missed your flight? Surely all staff could simply ask customers

when they order whether they are in a hurry and whether they want the bill fast or later? Simple – in fact, they just need to use common sense.

A simple lesson I learnt in my days of banking was to tell staff that if the systems are down when customers come into the bank, just take their numbers and call them with the required information when the systems are back up again. To do these things well is not difficult, but it requires a degree of initiative.

In conclusion

Marketing communications and sales are the two most visible elements of brand management. As such, they deserve much attention.

Most companies can get away with smaller budgets if they focus their efforts and make all they do task driven. Budgets do tend to get a life of their own in large companies.

The way in which we need to review the marketing communications for a brand is by answering questions like the following:

- What messages do I use to convey the brand positioning?
- Are the messages simple and easy to understand and relate to?
- Do I give consumers substantive reasons to believe my claims?
- Are they expressed in a creative way that has impact?
- Do I adhere to my brand's tone or personality?

- Do the media channels chosen reach the desired target audiences?
- Do the media channels complement one another?

- Do they include social media, and how do I manage that?

Does integrated marketing work? Brilliantly, if done well.

TWELVE

DELIVERING THE BRAND

- Most companies waste a lot of money selling to customers in marketing, and do very little to service their customers well

- Understand how everything translates into how you treat customers

- Most companies can't even begin to think about "a branded customer experience" if the most basic service experience is so bad

- There is a very low correlation between customer satisfaction and customer retention and growth

- Unless people in the company are all aligned to the same value system, they will not deliver the required brand experience

Despite the importance of great sales messages and great marketing communications, people really buy brands to satisfy their needs and wants. They buy a brand to enjoy the benefits that the brand offers. So, ultimately, a brand must deliver what it promises.

This means that a product must satisfy its customers' expectations. It must deliver the quality of experience the consumer expects and pays for. I have seen the sales of companies wax and wane on the basis of bad product quality.

Companies such as Proctor & Gamble, Toyota, Honda and Unilever are iconic in their belief that product quality is the most important component in the experience they deliver to consumers.

Product quality is sacrosanct in most markets, unless the industry is fully commoditised, such as in the US airline industry, or in market segments that want to pay less for less (for example, Tata cars). Yet, even in commoditised industries, there are often opportunities (as seen in airlines such as Etihad and Emirates). In many industries, actual product integrity alone may not be able to explain lower margins (for example Samsung versus Apple).

In Diagram 8, I list the questions a marketer should ask about product and service quality.

DIAGRAM 8
PRODUCT AND SERVICE QUALITY RELATIVE TO
BRAND POSITIONING: TYPICAL QUESTIONS

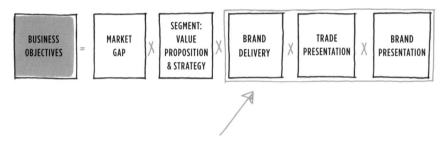

- Relative brand performance: Is there an opportunity?
- Relative brand performance in value/price.
- Rate of reccomendation. If existing. The nett promoter score (NPS).
- Expert and external evaluations. Speak to independent people such as specialists, suppliers and the media.

We know that product quality is a fundamental requirement for brand success, in the same way that the delivery of quality service is required for brand success. Yet, despite years of focus on quality management, quality standards, service quality management and lately customer experience, it remains one area most companies get wrong.

 I have always believed it's brand experience, not marketing, that can kill brands. Consumers will stay with a brand despite advertising they do not like. They will hardly defect because of that. But they will defect if their needs are not satisfied.

The brand must deliver on consumer expectations at every contact point the consumers have with it. This means that all components of a brand must be aligned for a brand to deliver a given value proposition to its customers.

Adamson states that for a brand to succeed the business strategy and staff must be aligned to the brand idea. Alignment means the ways in which:
- Staff are recruited and trained and the way they perform their jobs;
- The systems and administrative procedures of the brand work;
- The systems of the brand work to support its value proposition; and
- The infrastructure of the brand works to support its value proposition.

This is best achieved when brand owners deconstruct their value proposition to the consumer to determine what has to be done about systems, processes and people to deliver on the brand promise at every level of interface with the consumer.

The importance of customer service

The quality of both product and service must be such that brands retain and grow their customer base. In both cases we need to understand what customers expect, and ensure that we deliver that when and where they interface with our brand.

Product quality can be managed according to agreed standards of manufacturing and quality control. This is more difficult for service brands because their delivery is done at many contact points, with different people delivering it and in different places. A case in point is banks. Although they do a lot of training, most of them suffer from negative service experiences by their customers.

In the second senior marketing job of my life, I learnt many important lessons about customer service. I was manager for marketing information at Volkskasbank, today Absa. The general manager of marketing at that time, Stander Jordaan, a man who I respect to this day, insisted that we track every single customer who left the bank to find out why.

Even though I hated running a call centre, we started one (called Action Line). It worked. Customers called in large numbers. It took us a while to be able to handle the number of calls. We also sent postal questionnaires to all customers who moved their accounts to another bank to ask them why. I personally had to call all defecting clients with balances larger than R1 million.

We got many of these clients back because we showed that we cared. I learnt that marketing is not a theory. By talking and listening to customers, you learn what you need to know. That is why I cannot understand why some call centres are not managed by marketing departments.

Marketers need to know, on the ground, why they gain and lose customers. This is the most vital job of marketing. All else simply adds up to that. Tracking research, advertising testing, segmentation or any other kind of research is important. This research should support the decisions we make. Unless marketers know whether they gain or lose customers, and why, it is easy to become removed from the real job of marketing – identifying and satisfying customer needs. I have had many such debates with clients later on in my life. It is shocking how many marketers dismiss this point.

At the same time, I learnt that you have to understand the data to interpret it correctly.

We kept on losing customers because of bad customer service, although the bank invested a fortune on technology and staff training. Having just completed my doctorate, I made no sense of this because we adhered to the right principles I had been taught. So I decided to investigate it. I talked to 40 bank managers.

Firstly, 70% of the customer service complaints could be tracked back to being refused credit facilities. Customers do not like being told they cannot get credit so they call it bad service.

Secondly, a bank manager had to, on average, adhere to 41 steps in the process of credit evaluation and approval. This could take several weeks for smaller branches. So even if a bank manager wanted to service a loyal customer well, he could do it only by putting his own job on the line by overruling procedures.

Things are not always as simple as they seem. This is a lesson that I learnt over and over.

When 20twenty, the first online bank in South Africa, was launched many years later, CEO and founder Christo Davel designed the entire company around his value proposition to customers. The bank attracted a record number of customers faster than any South African bank to date. The service levels were exceptional.

Even when 20twenty was put under curatorship as part of its parent company, the bank retained 45 000 of its 50 000 customers for two more years. The customer service at the bank was so exceptional that customers stayed, even when they technically could lose money. I saw their views expressed online at the time. Customers did not want to leave because they did not believe any other bank would be as good. That is real loyalty and commitment.

Living the brand

Over the past few years, the concept of "living the brand" has become an important topic in its own right. As brands have become increasingly commoditised, it is clear that simply relying on exceptional service, even if few do it well, is not enough. The brand has to deliver an experience that is unique and in line with the expectations of its customers.

For a branded customer experience you have to dissect the contact points a customer will have with a brand and then design the appropriate experience at each one of these touch points, based on the customer expectation and the brand positioning.

Emirates does this very well. Staff are trained to behave in a certain way at each contact point with the customer. This means the brand becomes entirely experience based, and although it still faces competition, consumers now buy a unique experience particular to the given brand.

Starbucks also does this well. Each one of the stores is similar and uses a set of templates that is scaled for the location. The atmosphere is homely, welcoming and smells of good coffee. The concept is loosely based on an Italian espresso bar experience, but it is Americanised because the Italian experience is so particular to Italy and may not work elsewhere.

The coffee names endorse the experience, and the coffee machine and making process is visible. The aroma of the coffee endorses the experience. For travellers, Starbucks is almost a home from home where they can relax, check their emails with the free internet service and eat the kinds of goodies they can eat at home.

Yet, with all these different concepts like customer service, an on-brand experience and living the brand, which are important and how do they all work together? I believe they are all important, and are simply different sides of the same coin. All must work together to build up a unique customer experience that cannot simply be replicated by another brand. Arguably, great customer service can be copied by another brand, but a branded experience cannot.

The challenge is that most companies cannot even begin to think about a branded customer experience if the most basic service experience is so bad. We need to work at it with people, systems, processes and infrastructure to do it not only better, but also different, as Hamel also states. Yet very few companies do that.

I have always believed in a tiered way to connect these different concepts. Start with the easiest one but make all these concepts work together.

To explain: most companies deliver customer service that does not meet customer expectations. Although they may try to address it, most customer

experiences, despite staff training, will still be erratic and unsatisfactory. This means there will be a fair number of customer defections, regardless of all these activities.

Even if customers are satisfied, we also know that it does not mean they will not defect or not spread their suppliers. Most surveys indicate there is a very low correlation between customer satisfaction and customer retention and growth. It is because of the way the questions are asked, but it is also often because customers do not feel they are disloyal if they consider other options. They simply consider their options. This means that loyalty and retention programmes may often cost the company money, rather than lead to increased revenue, lower churn and higher profit margins.

Given this equation, a brand must go far beyond customer satisfaction to retain and grow customers. When we combine customer satisfaction with a unique brand experience and a well thought-through loyalty programme, we can start leveraging the brand and increase revenue and profit margins.

In South Africa, FNB is combining excellent customer service, unique products and competitive bank charges with its eBucks loyalty programme. In the process it is increasing its impact in the market, its customer growth and its customer retention. In recent years, the bank has increased its brand awareness and saliency, and its market share because of these initiatives.

In Diagram 9, I outline how I see the relationship between the different concepts used today to denote aspects of customer service and brand engagement.

DIAGRAM 9

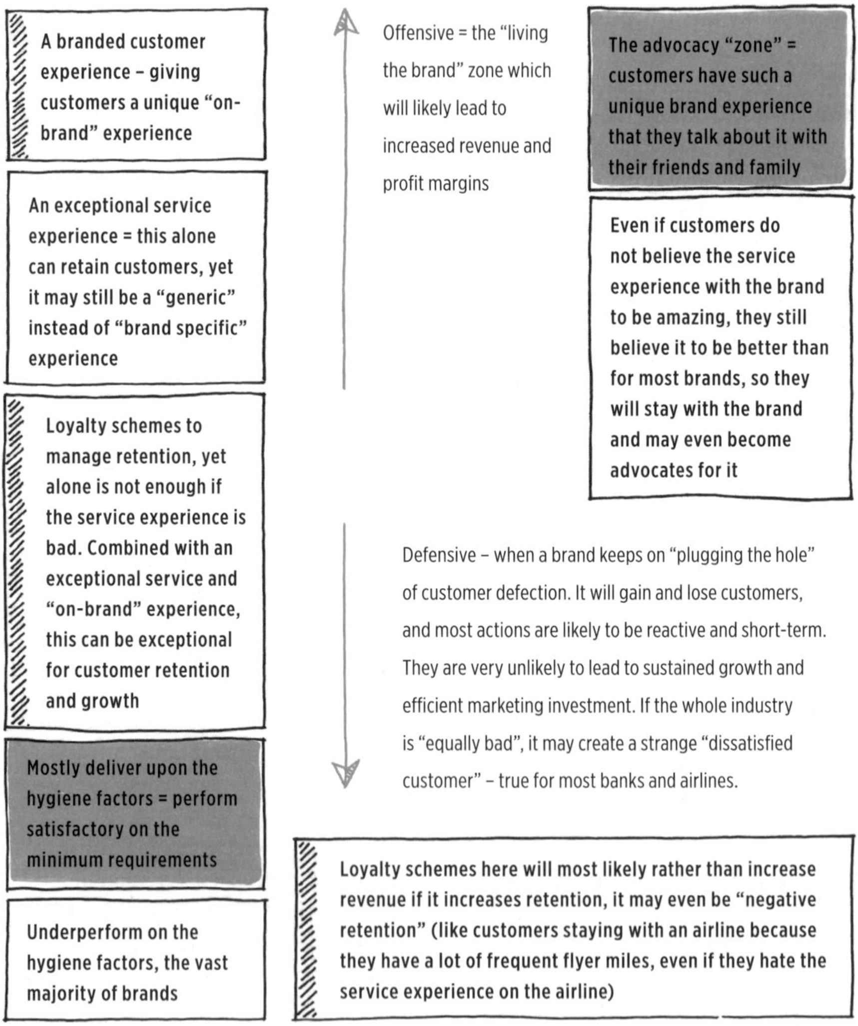

A branded customer experience – giving customers a unique "on-brand" experience

An exceptional service experience = this alone can retain customers, yet it may still be a "generic" instead of "brand specific" experience

Loyalty schemes to manage retention, yet alone is not enough if the service experience is bad. Combined with an exceptional service and "on-brand" experience, this can be exceptional for customer retention and growth

Mostly deliver upon the hygiene factors = perform satisfactory on the minimum requirements

Underperform on the hygiene factors, the vast majority of brands

Offensive = the "living the brand" zone which will likely lead to increased revenue and profit margins

The advocacy "zone" = customers have such a unique brand experience that they talk about it with their friends and family

Even if customers do not believe the service experience with the brand to be amazing, they still believe it to be better than for most brands, so they will stay with the brand and may even become advocates for it

Defensive – when a brand keeps on "plugging the hole" of customer defection. It will gain and lose customers, and most actions are likely to be reactive and short-term. They are very unlikely to lead to sustained growth and efficient marketing investment. If the whole industry is "equally bad", it may create a strange "dissatisfied customer" – true for most banks and airlines.

Loyalty schemes here will most likely rather than increase revenue if it increases retention, it may even be "negative retention" (like customers staying with an airline because they have a lot of frequent flyer miles, even if they hate the service experience on the airline)

How the business is structured, organised, managed and staffed endorses the delivery of the brand.

I have been fortunate to be involved in the early and launch phases of several new companies. Some of them have become significant brands with high awareness and stature in the marketplace. These include Outsurance (the first direct short-term insurer in South Africa), e.tv (the first free-to-air TV station in South Africa), McCarthy Call-A-Car (the largest online automotive retailer in South Africa) and 20twenty (the first online bank in South Africa).

In all these instances, the companies were aligned to deliver a given value proposition to customers – which leads to a lean, delivery-focused machine that runs efficiently.

Such a process aligns the following internal resources and processes:
- The values of the company;
- The way staff are recruited;
- The way the company is structured and the management is appointed;
- The way systems, procedures, administration and governance are designed;
- The way staff are incentivised and their key performance indicators devised; and
- The way company performance is measured.

Christo Davel taught me a simple fact during the launch of 20twenty. It starts with the right values. Unless people in the company are all aligned to the same value system, it will not work in the long term.

Adrian Gore, CEO and founder of Discovery, one of the most innovative companies in South Africa with operations in many other countries, told me that even though Discovery's concept of a lifestyle-based medical aid was unique at the time, its value system gave it a certain edge. He believes Discovery

would have prevailed even with a lesser concept.

Trevor Munday, then the deputy CEO of Sasol, told me the same many years ago. The inherent culture and value system of Sasol made it uniquely innovative in many areas.

Today Apple is the "poster child" of this principle. The inherent value system of Apple runs through how it works and all it does.

Yet, many companies do not get this. They believe using words like "innovation", "best practice", re-organisation", or "change management" will change a faulty value system. Either people are totally committed or they are not.

Let me use a simple example. Many years ago, our Durban branch of the agency FCB handled the advertising for the Three Cities Hotels. This group owned and ran iconic properties such as the Carlton in Johannesburg, the Royal in Durban and The Peninsula in Cape Town. All three hotels were exceptional in every way.

The then chairman was so committed to excellence that he flew in red roses from Israel every week when these were not available in South Africa. Each table in each restaurant had one red rose on it. This became one of his trademark elements. He also imported very fine-grained sand to be used to form the imprints in his lift lobby ashtrays.

Some will call these things extreme, and granted they are, but they do show a certain commitment to being exceptional in what you do

I remember watching Sol Kerzner, CEO of the One & Only Resorts Group, walking around outside the One & Only Royal Mirage in Dubai one morning while I was having breakfast. Even though he ran the whole group, he still checked the small details of his hotels – whether the lawn was cut well, whether the breakfast display was faultless.

The point was made a while ago that Steve Jobs of Apple was interested in even the minute detail of the way a headphone worked. It demonstrates a certain commitment to quality. Some may associate this with lunacy, but to me it demonstrates a philosophy and a way of doing things.

 The right value system starts at the top. It has to be a way of life. It is not something that can be taught through value programmes, even though these may help to support the message throughout the organisation. Real values are not just nice words printed onto posters, like "trust" or "integrity".

Today I am again fortunate to be involved in two such start-up companies, one in the life insurance business and one in the financial services and money management business. In each instance, the company is being devised according to the value proposition to its customers. Not only is it hugely rewarding, it shows that marketing is the business.

Such a business is usually also efficient, because it focuses on efficient and effective delivery to customers. The company has only as many resources in any one area as are required to deliver to customers and operate efficiently.

Usually the management is also clear on the focus and what is required. The company does not focus on fixing mistakes but on one output. Often de-constructing the value proposition of the business can help, because most companies I have dealt with are over-engineered in many ways that add no significant customer value, sustainable competitive advantage, superior growth or profit margins, or any other meaningful advantage that will grow the asset value of the company.

Here are some typical questions to help you review delivery:
- Are my customers experiencing the brand they expect? Is their experience in line with the brand's positioning?
- Are my facilities and staff aligned?
- Does our brand deliver in the trade by being in stock where people want to buy it, and is it merchandised and displayed well?
- Does my brand deliver the quality that consumers expect?
- Is the delivery consistent?

THIRTEEN

MANAGING THE COSTS

○ Am I buying more brand awareness than my competitors for the same amount or less?

○ Stop brand declines before they become unstoppable

 It costs money to make money. That also applies to the process of creating a brand through all the steps to the point of brand delivery. In fact, considerable investment normally goes into launching, growing and maintaining a brand.

On the one hand, you are faced with the challenge of spending enough money to enable your brand marketing to succeed. On the other hand you must be careful not to overspend and not to spend unwisely.

A marketer has to manage the value of the brand, with the same or lesser resources. Whilst it is easy to splurge, clever marketing is far more efficient.

DIAGRAM 10
MANAGING COSTS

Create and manage at the same or lower cost than competitors

When you launch a brand with a significant new message, make sure that you spend enough money to make it work.

When I worked on the Colgate-Palmolive business many years ago at the agency, we launched the first micro-detergent in South Africa, called ABC. It was highly successful in Canada, and we knew it would work here. The client wanted to break into the detergent market, which at the time was dominated by Unilever with brands such as Omo, Surf and Skip.

The launch went very well. We had researched it and consumers really liked the idea. Yet, within weeks, Unilever converted all its brands into micro-detergents, completely undermining our first-mover advantage with dominance of media spend and trade presence.

So even a great idea needs to be communicated well, because existing strong brands will do anything to protect their turf. This implies being aware that another brand may simply outspend you. If this is possible, can you respond effectively? It sometimes helps if you literally spend the entire budget fast to gain as much awareness as possible as fast as possible. It does create some barriers to entry.

Brands such as Proctor & Gamble and Unilever believe in the principle of dominance. When Proctor & Gamble launched its first shampoo in South Africa (Head & Shoulders), it spent to dominate. In a category that spent at the time only about R5 million on total advertising per year, Proctor & Gamble spent four times that amount in the first year. This, of course, created a huge barrier to entry for other brands, and no doubt it works to own a market.

The often-cited example of Toyota spending money both in recessionary times and in good times is true. This belief has sustained it as the leading brand in South Africa, even through very tough times.

A marketer I highly respect, Nick Griffin, for many years the marketing director of Avis in South Africa, believes in never spending less than 50% of the estimated category marketing spend. Whenever there was a new location that became important, Avis had to be there. He believed in being as close as possible to airport arrival areas and tourist facilities – the closer the better. I know he refused to take positions that did not offer Avis this kind of dominance.

Avis became the brand leader that way, and dominated the category with a market share of over 45%, despite having many competitors. Then Nick left, and Imperial relaunched as Europcar and started spending more on marketing. Today, I have no doubt that Europcar has gained significant market share away from Avis. Marketing spend is not a guarantee that a brand will do well, but it can help a lot.

Theoretically, it is easy to differentiate a brand by spending more than competitors do. For some brands it is possible to do that, but in most cases it is not. The challenge is mostly to spend effectively and efficiently, and to achieve more with less.

In all instances, a company has to achieve its set objectives with the resources available to it. On the basis of its performance, the value of its shares (and thus of the company) will increase. If it performs well, the growth for shareholders and other stakeholders will be good. It if does not perform well, the shareholders may eventually withdraw their support for the company and its management.

Good financial management is thus about how well a given set of resources is applied to grow the value of a company for its stakeholders. For some companies these resources will be considerable; for others, limited.

Critical mass will usually benefit the very large companies in that they can invest more in higher quality and greater numbers of staff, in the training of their staff, and in infrastructure and systems.

Companies in the same product or service category generally have access to similar resources. The companies that will do better are those that leverage their resources better than the others.

A company should do a full diagnostic evaluation to understand which of its facets are not contributing optimally to the process of value creation. A detailed diagnostic will enable the company to prioritise those operations and actions that are essential to achieve its objectives.

For example, if the company suffers from problems with brand awareness or brand perception, it needs to address its brand communications to solve the problem. If the brand under-delivers on the expectations of customers, it needs to evaluate its performance and address the issues of product quality or service quality. If the company is losing customers, it needs to address product and service quality issues.

If the company suffers from low profit margins, it will have to review its value proposition. Is it in line with customer needs and wants? Is there still a market there? Is competition just too strong and is the company a me-too player? Does the company perform and does it have

a quality perception? Does it pay a fair price for its raw materials and labour? Is it productive?

If the company simply sells low volumes but all else seems fine, its product (or service) may be unavailable where its customers want to buy it.

All in all, a company wants to achieve the same or more, with the same or fewer resources. And a proper review can clearly identify where the focus should be to rectify the brand problem.

The measurement of brand results is the ultimate measure of brand success. Typical questions to ask are:

- Who am I gaining and who am I losing as customers? Why?
- Am I gaining more than I am losing? Why?
- Are target-market consumers aware of my brand? If not, why not? And if they are, what do they say about my brand? How does that differentiate my brand from others, if at all?
- Do customers try out my brand? If so, do they keep on buying it after trial? If not, why not?
- Are my users happy with my brand? If not, why not? Do they extend their usage in my brand space? If not, why not? Do they recommend my brand to others? If not, why not?
- What is my market share? Is it growing? If not, why not?
- What is the trend of profit margin for my brand against the market average? Does it increase or decrease? Why?
- Is the market I am in growing? If so, am I getting my share of the growth?

- Are there market segments that are under-penetrated? How do I fare in the different segments?
- What is the asset value of my brand? Is it growing? If not, why not?
- Am I doing this at the same costs or less than competitors?
- How can I index my own brand efficiency and effectiveness against competitors? Why am I doing better or worse?

When evaluating the actual input costs of a brand, ratios are useful in determining whether we are buying more value than the money we pay. Let me illustrate this:

- All we do in marketing must translate into what we pay for what we get.
- Am I buying more brand awareness than my competitors for the same amount or less?
- Am I buying desirable brand benefits (desirable relative to what I set as my brand objectives) – more so than my competitors for the same money, or less?
- Can my target-market customers tell me what my brand stands for when I ask them?
- Do target-market consumers talk about my brand more than they do about the brands of my competitors?
- Am I buying a greater predisposition of non-customers to use my brand for the same amount or less money?
- Do I have more loyal and committed customers than my competitors?
- Will more of my customers recommend my brand over those of my competitors?
- Is my brand in decline on any of these factors?

It is easy to reverse a decline before it accelerates. It is far more difficult once it has gone too far. As with Malcolm Gladwell's tipping point, a negative tipping point is as destructive as a positive tipping point is constructive. Yet, I often find marketers who dismiss signals of decline.

I find these questions important navigational stars on the road to brand value. If you are on top of these, with the same or less marketing spend, you are doing well.

FOURTEEN

LOOKING BACK TO

KEEP MOVING FORWARD

> Research is often seen as the black sheep of marketing

> If marketing material does not scare you a little,
> it is unlikely to have any impact

> It is not what the research says but how we interpret it and what
> we do with it that matters

I am a great believer in measurement to enable us to keep moving in the right direction. Especially because marketing is by its very nature subjective, we need to make sure that whatever we do will work.

I was fortunate to start my marketing life in research. This gave me a foundation that I will always be thankful for. It is a pity that research is often seen as the black sheep of marketing, when proper research is a fundamental aspect of it. Even though I agree with people such as Steve Jobs, who said that researching consumer needs in traditional ways hardly ever comes up with something new, there are places where research can be a very powerful tool if used well.

I was also fortunate to be able to conduct the first ever needs-based segmentation in South Africa in the middle eighties, a few years after the technique was conceived of by Russell Haley. It was amazing to see how data fell into place. We could identify locally the life-stage segments as advocated by the Stanford Research Institute at the time.

 Volkskasbank taught me the importance of using the internal customer data of a company in conjunction with research at a time when this was still done rarely. Even though the data contained a lot of mistakes, it was much better than no data. We just needed to apply common sense to it.

I remember identifying that black people made up a much larger portion of the customers of the bank than anyone in management had thought. This led us to conduct consumer research to identify why black clients banked with us, allowing us to start targeting black people more aggressively.

Together with Sasol Oil, we initiated the first continuous brand-tracking research in South Africa, conducting fieldwork every day of the week for 50 weeks a year. The reason I am so sure it was the first is that no local research company wanted to do it. A small research company, called Carnelly Rangecroft, agreed to do it (and proved to be exceptional people to work with). Today, every large company does continuous tracking as a matter of course.

We used the tracking to plan the impact of campaigns and all the media exposure of Sasol Oil, airing the commercials that gave us the best value for money. The tracking enabled us to stretch the marketing budget. We all learnt that the right research is invaluable.

We also conducted a lot of research to know the brand and what it stood for – so much so that anyone in the company could immediately identify whether a campaign was on-brand. To this day, few companies are able to do that. We made many great campaigns with Sasol, and understanding the brand so well made it much easier for all of us.

Sasol Oil was an exceptional company to deal with. If you wanted more marketing money, you needed to prove that what you had would work. It is hard to work with engineers if you are a marketer – but this experience proved very valuable to me in later years.

I will always remember that however rigorous the argument was, they always respected you as being on their side and arguing to make things better. Such clients are rare. I can understand why Sasol is listed as one of the Top 50 future giants from emerging markets – and the only South African one – in the book *The Emerging Markets Century* by Antoine van Agtmael.

When we launched the first Yebo Gogo campaign at the FCB agency for Vodacom, we did a lot of research into the key factors that people expect from a mobile service provider. We worked directly with Alan Knott-Craig. He was a visionary and set very high demands on suppliers. This campaign became the cornerstone that built the Vodacom brand, and even though I can only

claim to have been instrumental in researching what matters to consumers, we all felt proud of what we achieved.

We also realised that we needed a strong television presence to counter the strong radio property of MTN at the time. Again, this worked. We tracked the campaign and within four months or so, we overtook MTN in brand awareness.

Alan Knott-Craig was clear that Vodacom had to be the brand and market leader, and for that it needed to be the best in its class: the best network, the best airtime sales coverage and the best brand. He details these areas in his autobiography. I remember when we presented the follow-up commercial after the Yebo Gogo commercial had been aired for some weeks. We did not retain anything from the Yebo Gogo commercial, looking for something better.

However Alan insisted that we bring those elements, like the Yebo Gogo phrase, back into our advertising. He understood the fundamental importance of consistency in building a brand. Even if at times I felt the story dragged on for long enough, it still worked to make Vodacom an iconic South African brand.

Although MTN and Sasol are the two South African companies that I respect most, the brand consistency and "South African-ness" of Vodacom had a lot to do with its success over the years. This has clearly been lost today, creating an opportunity for the other networks.

The problem of pre-testing

I have found advertising pre-testing fairly dangerous over the years. I really do not like asking a sample of consumers what they think of an ad before it is made, even though I have done pre-testing hundreds of times and understand all the arguments for and against it – and can understand why marketers want to do it. Logically, it makes sense to have greater certainty before you act. Yet I believe doing a lot of upfront exploratory research is of far greater value as it can explore creative directions and options even before concepts are tested.

One key problem with pre-testing is that consumers are conditioned to expect certain things (such as cars in car advertising), so it becomes difficult for them to make the mindset leap when they are exposed to a concept that is different in a prototype format. Great concepts get culled in the process.

Why scary advertising?

My acid test for advertising is always this: if it does not scare you a little, it is too safe and is unlikely to have any impact on the market. In a world where we need to buy more bang for our buck, impact is the greatest leverage factor we have in marketing. Marketers are often far too scared to make slightly dangerous decisions, resulting in blandness and low efficiency.

Although 10% or more of consumers dislike a great piece of marketing, you have to live with it. It is part of the game. The only way never to make a mistake is to do nothing at all. That I learnt from my CEO at Volkskasbank when I was in my twenties, a great man called Koot van Vuuren.

Of course you can take risk too far. When I worked on the ABSA business in the early days of that bank, we made a commercial for homeloans showing a pen turning into a snake. The message was: make sure you know what you are signing for at other banks as it may turn around and bite you. We had to withdraw this commercial after two airings. It was simply seen as too aggressive. In fact, one of the most risky areas for a brand is aggression. Very few can do it and get away with it. Irreverence, however, can be very powerful.

To decide how best to launch a new brand, or how to assess the position of a current brand to enable us to manage it better, we can use the model outlined above. This model will indicate what areas within the brand must get the most attention, by which I mean where the current breakdowns in brand delivery are. It will also indicate the areas that will give us most leverage to strengthen the brand.

What kinds of research work for me? Here are some pointers:
- What drives the market in volume and value of consumption;
- Knowledge of our competitors;
- What our consumers want and need, and how that differs between groups of consumers;
- How well our brand stacks up in awareness and perceptions and how this differs by segment and in those segments that are important to us;

- Whether our brand is talked about and whether customers recommend it to others;
- Research to generate the language consumers use when they talk about our category, the brands and the marketing;
- Research to test a new product;
- Whether people saw our advertising and what it told them;
- How people buy – their decision-making and buying;
- What people buy;
- The performance of our brand against others;
- How satisfied our customers are with our brand; and
- A first impression of advertising ideas or concepts. (This is more useful than pre-testing, which happens late in the day and is fraught with variables you cannot control.)

What can't we expect from research?

Research does not make decisions. It provides us with the information to make decisions more easily, to reduce uncertainty in what we decide. Many people use research like a crutch. It does not take away our responsibility as marketers and executives, but it can assist us.

Know the limitations of what consumers can tell you. It is not their job to interpret what can be done with new technology. We have to use our insights and observations to devise products and services they want. They will hardly ever give us definitive input we can use to innovate. A very good qualitative researcher will get a lot more out through interpretation and reading between the lines. Sadly, most qualitative research does not do that.

Product tests are hardly ever definitive, so I am not always sure what they tell us other than to confuse us more.

Always remember that whoever does research will largely get the same or similar answers. It is not what the research says that matters, it is how we interpret it and what we ultimately do with it that matters.

Research is invaluable if used well to guide decisions, but it needs to be combined with insight, experience and an aptitude for risk at management level. The right research opens up opportunities, it does not limit them.

FIFTEEN

GAINING WITHOUT LOSING

- Know and build the core values of your brand

- Category values do not differentiate the brand. They simply illustrate functionality

- Use peripheral values to modernise your brand

- Lego started developing products far beyond its traditional strengths, leaving gaps for lower-priced competitors

- Old Spice retained its core values but adapted to a new generation of users

Many marketers struggle with the question of how to evolve a brand and retain its modernity without alienating current consumers. I believe part of the reason is that we do not really try to understand what makes our brand successful (or not successful). Once we know this, we will also know how to retain high-value customers and attract new customers in ways that are still true to the brand.

It is important to know what elements should be retained in the way a given brand is portrayed. Retaining these elements will make customers recognise their brand immediately when they see it. Changing these elements may alienate existing customers, but it may also cause consumers to confuse one brand with another.

This kind of consistency used to be fairly simplistic. Brands retained elements such as colours, sounds, people and approach. We know, for instance, that Rolex uses famous people as endorsements, the assumption being that an exceptional person has the discernment to wear a Rolex watch. Similarly, a brand may retain a visual device, like the Michelin Man, which aids immediate brand recognition.

Today, this kind of consistency is often more subtle – it is mainly attitudinal. We know a Virgin Atlantic advertisement because the brand uses a certain unique tone. Within seconds of seeing a Virgin advertisement on television, you know the advertisement is for Virgin.

This kind of recognition factor is very valuable for a brand, because it means you buy immediate brand recognition. Not only does it endorse the uniqueness of the brand, it also means the exposure of the advertisement is economical and efficient.

An article about Lego in *Bloomberg Business Week* on 23 July 2010 endorses the importance of knowing what a brand stands for and evolving within its confines. In the late 1990s, Lego started developing products that contradicted its heritage of building blocks that could be assembled and re-assembled into many different models and applications with a fair degree of building skill and imagination.

Essentially, Lego veered away from its core values as a brand and into the product territories already occupied by many other toy manufacturers. Lego started developing products that stretched far from its traditional strengths. The Galidor line of action figures, for example, could be assembled and re-assembled only with huge difficulty. In the process, Lego left gaps for lower-priced competitors to enter the market.

On the other hand, Lego got it right later when the City Fire Truck, an iconic Lego piece, was redesigned in 2005 to look like an authentic fire truck, not a stylised version of it. By 2008 it was again the top seller in the Lego product range.

The Lego brand name encapsulates the values that define the brand, but the evolution of product design within the framework of Lego's value set keeps the brand relevant to the needs of today's consumer and authentic to the Lego brand.

Adamson uses the example of how his agency pitched for the Nikon advertising account. At the time, Nikon wanted to capture a portion of the point-and-shoot camera market into which Canon and Minolta were making inroads, but it wanted to do so without jeopardising the core values of Nikon as the camera used by serious professional photographers. It came up with the brand driver line of "approachable authority".

Retaining the core values of a brand is vital in any brand extension, in particular in deciding how far a brand can stretch.

Brands operate at three distinct levels:

First, the **core level**, comprising the key aspects of a brand that set it apart from other brands. These elements, cited for Lego and Nikon above, are deeply rooted and mostly appeal to the deepest human needs, wants, aspirations and desires. These values never change for a brand. In fact, changing them would undermine the brand because it would become alien to its existing user base.

Second, the **category level** that pertains to functionality. The best way to explain this is that most brand communications contain elements of the category. Shampoo advertising will show how people wash and vigorously shake their hair to demonstrate how well it cleans and shines hair.

None of these aspects generally differentiate the brands, they purely demonstrate and educate the consumer about usage – and unless the brand is the first mover in a category in a new market, it is arguable whether it adds value to the brand.

Third, the **peripheral level**, comprising the aspects of the brand that keep it current, such as music, fashions, venues, colours, and sports stars or other celebrities. These change from time to time and so have the ability to keep a brand up to date and contemporary.

Let us outline these.

The core values of your brand

A brand has a set of core values that are deeply rooted in human needs, wants, desires and emotions. For historically fast-moving consumer goods brands, it may be pure functionality, which is often connected to deeper emotions or psychological benefits.

In the first (or primary) place, a good detergent may do its primary job well: to wash laundry clean and make it suitable for wearing again. At a deeper level, it may be the feeling of comfort (or, for some, even security) from having performed domestic chores well and having the approval of family members.

For personal products such as shampoo and perfume, these benefits will vary greatly. At their most basic level, these products will benefit people in making them look and smell clean. At another level the product will make them feel good about themselves and confident enough to mingle with others they may be interested in as friends or lovers. At further levels, it will make others take notice of them and may even make them feel attractive to others.

All these products operate at more than one level.

 In a way, a brand is like a mirror that we hold up. We form a unique bond with it that we ourselves may not even consider particularly important but that gives us a degree of comfort. This may be using the bank that our parents used or using the toothpaste that we grew up with or going to a holiday destination that we visited with our family.

Even though we may have such a comfort zone with some products that we buy them without even thinking, they may have become part of a set of associations that are deeply seated in childhood when our parents looked after us. For that reason, consumers can often not say why they use certain products.

It is safe to say that the more our brand behaviour mirrors our emotional equilibrium, the more satisfied we may be with our purchases. A brand fit will be subconscious, although we may think it irrelevant or unimportant to people.

The deepest level of human emotions relates to the deeper emotions associated with brands. This may be explicit (functionality) or it may be implicit (emotional reward). In most instances it is likely to be both.

Many brands have very clear core values. Historically, perfume brands used them blatantly: glamorous female models in suggestive underwear and a suggestive posture. Male models are often used in naked or semi-naked poses, with suggestive commentary and even phallic symbols.

Johnny Walker still uses the "walking man", once a very outdated brand identity but today applied in many unique ways that extend the core values of the brand. The logo of the brand has been used to create a new language for the brand. This is very powerful as it retains the DNA of the brand throughout without boring consumers.

As markets mature, core values become even more important: stick to your roots because they add an aura of stability and security amid change. A leading brand's identification with its roots also makes it difficult for competitors to try to erode its strength.

The category values of your brand

Category values relate to the functional usage of brands. A car gets you from point A to B. Cellphones keep you in touch with significant others in your life. Shampoo cleans hair. Detergents clean laundry. ABS brakes on a car are a standard in the industry today and are no longer a differentiator. These are all basic performance benefits.

Category values are often also the visual depictions of brands: advertising that shows cars in car ads, even when a car is very similar – or looks very similar – to others in the same class. These may be useful for educating consumers of first-mover brands entering new markets but they do not add value beyond that. These values do not differentiate the brand. They simply illustrate functionality.

I have seen the danger of this. If a brand does not lead and uses only category symbols in its marketing, it is often confused with larger brands. This may mean the marketing works more for the leading brand, which is a downright waste of money and shows we, the marketers, have not done our homework to determine what sets our brand apart from competitors.

How to keep a brand modern or relevant

At the third level there are peripheral values. Although human needs remain the same, many things in society change regularly, and a brand needs to adapt to these changes to remain relevant and to communicate to consumers in relevant ways. We may also need to express core values in new ways to attract new users.

The fast rate of change in society, with reference to the mass media, new trends, the rapid growth of emerging economies, the growth of social media and the general availability of information everywhere and anywhere, means that brands now have to adapt faster.

At this level, we talk about peripheral values: those values that change from year to year. Typical examples are colours, music, fashions and food.

A great brand evolution

A very good example of a successful brand evolution is Old Spice, which retained the core values that matter but adapted to a new generation of users.

I remember working on the Old Spice brand about 20 years ago. Even then, Old Spice was not the kind of after-shave lotion or deodorant most young males would use. Yet in its core market it was iconic. It was the generic brand in its category.

The brand was old-fashioned and inexpensive. This was endorsed by its crude plastic and red packaging, which may have been modern for its time. It was inexcusably male. Its values endorsed this. Today, it would probably be considered chauvinistic. We talked, even then, about how we could make the brand appeal to younger users. Yet, we never succeeded.

Old Spice made no excuses for what it was – the brand that older males would buy. The older users were not interested in the new brands launched at the time (such as Aramis). These brands were much more expensive and more sophisticated in their imagery. They often used black-and-white photography, soft lighting and beautiful models. They had a distinctive air of one-upmanship. The sex appeal was often explicit.

Against this, Old Spice was boring. It had no sex appeal beyond its crude maleness. In imagery terms it was similar to Marlboro and Camel cigarettes. Yet, through its straightforward maleness, it had enormous sex appeal.

The new brands were everything that Old Spice was not.

Old Spice believed there would always be a market for its brand – a market that would not fall for the sophisticated imagery and higher price. The consumers of Old Spice needed to smell good, but at a price they were prepared to pay. One can even argue that the fragrance of Old Spice was crude compared with the newcomers, yet this is what its consumers preferred.

In this context, its new creative work was conceived. It is still the brand it always was, but its campaign expresses it in a contemporary way. The new campaign has all the elements that make the brand unique. The models are as male as male can be. Yet they deliberately make fun of these males in a way most people would find appealing. And while the campaign uses sex appeal, it does so in a light-hearted and hyperbolic way – which is the right tone in a contemporary society where the line between the sexes is often blurred. It tells us being male is still OK. And we can even make fun of our own peculiarities. It reminds us of the great line *Men's Health* used, "Guy stuff".

CONCLUSION

I hope this book has given you some direction and some ideas of how to manage your brands and your marketing so that it is more goal-directed, efficient and effective. If you picked up just one idea from this book, I would be grateful.

In the above approach, we outline the areas we can assess to ascertain how best to launch or manage our brands in the most efficient and effective way.

This tool can be used as a diagnostic that will enable better management of a brand. It will also enable the longer-term alignment of all aspects of a brand and create a clear template for everyone who works on the brand, resulting in easier and better brand briefs and brand output.

Ultimately, a well-integrated approach will create and build the value of your brand.

I will conclude by using my borrowed quote from Kurt Vonnegut: "Do something that scares you every day." Once you know the rules of marketing, break them.

Hardly anything significant has ever been done without a good mix of insight, analysis and creativity. Insight and analysis can only take you that far. After that, intuition and creativity take over. That is the hallmark of a great marketer.

ROLL OF HONOUR

Willie Rossouw, Andriesa Singleton and the exceptional management team of Sasol Oil, we had the scope to experiment with different exposure patterns to optimise the money spent. Hannes Botha, Lean Strauss, Ernst Oberholtzer, Charles Steyn and Andre van der Merwe always challenged us in a positive and inspiring way.

When we launched McCarthy Call-A-Car, we had two great clients in Louwrens Botha and Brand Pretorius, who were prepared to experiment but who also had a lot of marketing common sense.

My client at Battery Centre, a great businessman called Louis Loubser, and his marketer, Robyn Liston, were both common-sense marketing people.

The former CEO of Polyfin, Trevor Munday, could not control market circumstances, such as the oil price, but he and his executive demonstrated a superior ability to understand these and create superior value for the company.

Our client for the launch of e.tv, Jonathan Proctor, was a true visionary and an amazing man to work with. To him marketing was the business, so the agency was involved in every single thing they did.

Working with MTN across most of its operations in Africa and the Middle East, for eight years now, have exposed me to over 700 of the very best marketing brains in the region, facing an extraordinary array of challenges. MTN have allowed me, through their previous Global CMO Santie Botha, to validate many of the concepts outlined herein.

Working on a brand like Emirates for many years, seeing how a global brand takes shape from a strong, central vision. How the entire brand gets aligned with the vision of its chairman

We worked with a large team of suppliers for the merger of Comparex and Business Connexion. Everyone in the team was managed with a firm hand by Diana de Souza, a highly capable client.

Back in the middle eighties, Clive Corder and Hanna Fourie of Market Research Africa researched for me the first needs-based segmentation in South Africa.

Erik du Plessis of Milward Brown and Butch Rice of Research Surveys both taught me a lot.

My first two bosses in the real world, Irene Haymes of Colgate and Stander Jordaan of Volkskas Bank allowed me to make mistakes but were great leaders.

Christo Davel and René Otto, two iconic South African business visionaries, were inspiring to work with.

Margie King and Charles Naude for editing.

Breinstorm Brand Architects for the invaluable insights and the design of the final product.

My friend and colleague of many years, the late Dr Klaas Jonkheid, who told me in 1993 that the internet will still rule marketing – how right he was!

DR THOMAS OOSTHUIZEN

A marketing, brand & communications strategist that has worked for many global and local brands in Africa and the Middle East for over 30 years.

- Worked as a marketer (brand management, consumer research and marketing communications at Colgate-Palmolive & Volkskasbank, today part of ABSA) and a supplier to marketers (advertising and brand agencies, including Draft FCB).
- Doctorate in Marketing Communications from the University of South Africa.
- Extra-ordinary Professor in Business Management, University of Johannesburg.
- On the National Advisory Board of the Vega Brand School and a board member of the IIE of Advtech.
- Advertising Man of the Year, The Star newspaper, 2001.
- Past adjudicator for many global and local industry awards, including the Financial Mail, FinWeek, UAE IBDA Awards, Roger Garlick Media Award, the Outdoor Media Awards, the PRISA Awards & the American Advertising Efficiency Awards.
- On the Editorial Review Board of the Asia Pacific Management Review.
- In the top 5% most searched LinkedIn profiles globally.

EXPERIENCE HIGHLIGHTS

- Established an alternative form of integrated communications company, O2 Communications, with an average operating margin four times the industry average, with highly notable work done for clients like Emirates around the world.
- For over fourteen years, enabled Sasol Oil advertising to be the most liked and noted fuel advertising in South Africa.
- Compiled the entire launch communications strategy for the initial launch of AngloGold Ashanti on five continents and the New York Stock Exchange.
- Conducted the research and compiled the strategy that led to the Vodacom "Yebo Gogo" campaign eighteen years ago.
- Compiled the marketing, brand and communications strategy and launched Outsurance, today the largest consumer short term insurance brand in South Africa.
- Compiled the marketing planning template used by Emirates for its country operations. Developed many global campaigns for them as one of their lead agencies, O2.
- Compiled the brand strategy for MTN across Africa and the Middle East. Conducted the marketing and brand training for all their operations for five years.
- Conducted the marketing training for American clinical research company, Parexel. Compiled their divisional strategic marketing plan for 2013.
- Compiled the marketing, brand and communications strategy for e.tv, the largest free-to-air television station in South Africa, and launched it.

REFERENCES

Adamson, Allen, 2006, *Brand Simple,* Palgrave MacMillan, New York

Bonchek, Mark, 2013, Purpose is Good. Shared Purpose is Better. *Harvard Business Review* blog, available from http://blogs.hbr.org/cs/2013/03/purpose_is_good_shared_purpose.html

Davis, Scott, 2002, *Brand Asset Management,* Jossey-Bass, New York

Gladwell, Malcolm, 2000, *The Tipping Point*, Little, Brown, London

Greene, Jay, 2010, How Lego Revived its Brand, *Bloomberg Business Week,* 23 July 2010, available from http://www.businessweek.com/innovate/content/jul2010/id20100722_781838.htm

Hamel, Gary, 1998, *Creating the Future*, Kantola Productions, available from http://www.kantola.com/Dr-Gary-Hamel-PDPD-92-S.aspx

Johnson, Bill, The CEO of Heinz on Powering Growth, *Harvard Business Review,* October 2011

Kim, W Chan & Mauborgne, Renne, 2005, *Blue Ocean Strategy*, Harvard Business Press, Boston, Massachusetts

Levitt, Theodore, 1986, *The Marketing Imagination,* The Free Press, New York

Llopis, Glenn, 2011, The most Successful Companies Embrace the Promise of their Culture, *Forbes,* 12 September 2009, available from http://www.forbes.com/sites/glennllopis/2011/09/12/the-most-successful-companies-embrace-the-promise-of-their-culture/

Martin, Roger, 2009, *The Design of Business*, Harvard Business Press, Boston, Massachusetts

McDonald, Malcolm & Wilson, Hugh, 2007, *Marketing Plans: How to Prepare Them, How to Use Them*, Wiley, Chichester, UK

Moore, Geoffrey A, 1991 (1999), *Crossing the Chasm: Marketing and Selling High-Tech Products to Mainstream Customers*, HarperBusiness Essentials, New York

Neumeier, Marty, 2006, *The Brand Gap,* New Riders Publications, Berkeley, CA

Porter, Michael, 1996, What is Strategy?, *Harvard Business Review,* November–December 1996, available from http://hbr.org/1996/11/what-is-strategy

Reeves, Rosser, 1961, *Reality in Advertising*, Knopf, New York

Utterback, James, 2006, *Design-Inspired Innovation*, World Scientific Publishing Company, Singapore

Van Agtmael, Antoine, 2007, *The Emerging Markets Century: How a New Breed of World-Class Companies Is Overtaking the World*, Simon and Schuster, New York

Welch, Jack, 2012, JWMI: Jack Welch on Winning, MBA series clip on YouTube, available from http://www.youtube.com/watch?v=vyOQU6s2hdo